THE NEW RIGHT:
WE'RE READY TO LEAD

THE NEW RIGHT: WE'RE READY TO LEAD

RICHARD A. VIGUERIE

The Viguerie Company

ISBN: 0-9604814-1-9
Library of Congress Catalog Card No: 80-53101

Printed in the United States of America

Dedication

To my mother and father.

How can anyone ever adequately thank their parents for their love, sacrifice, understanding, guidance, direction, patience, their always helpful hand, all of which seems to flow without end?

From a grateful son—thank you.

Acknowledgements

I have been thinking about and collecting notes, articles and other matieral for this book for the past four years. I suddenly realized that the fall of 1980—when perhaps the most important presidential election in the 20th century will be held—was the time it should be published. I am indebted to many people for helping me publish this book on short notice.

I want to thank fellow conservatives Morton Blackwell, John Lofton, Howard Phillips, Jim Martin and Bill Rhatican for their suggestions and criticisms.

I have drawn heavily upon *Conservative Digest* and *The New Right Report* for many of the facts and figures which fill the book.

I wish to also acknowledge the help of John Coyne and Curt Smith. I am especially indebted for the editorial assistance of a very old friend, Lee Edwards, without whose help this book would not have been possible.

INTRODUCTION
BY JERRY FALWELL

At this present hour, there can be no questioning the retrogression of America's stability as a free and healthy nation. In the last several years, Americans have literally stood by and watched as godless, spineless leaders have brought our nation floundering to the brink of death.

Too many of our top governmental officials, including judges in high place, legislators, bureaucrats, and politicians, have cared more about getting a vote than about courageously standing for what is right and good for America. Considering that the stability of any group, whether it be a family or a nation, rises and falls upon leadership, it is no wonder that we find America depraved, decadent, and demoralized today.

As a parent and as a God-fearing citizen, I respect Mr. Viguerie's courage to speak out regarding liberals and their actions that have significantly occasioned America's perilous condition. Mr. Viguerie speaks with candor. He is blunt and to the point. The vacuum of leadership in America must be filled. Conservative Americans must now take the helm and guide America back to a position of stability and greatness.

Granted that the writer is hardly wholly objective since he himself is one of the key figures in the New Right, nevertheless, I believe that the book provides insight into the thinking of men and women who are leading a movement which, if anything, has been underrated by the news media as to its ultimate impact in American politics.

Mr. Viguerie uses the term the "New Right" to speak of those moral citizens who now must come together and let their voice be heard, those, as he puts it:

"hard-working citizens sick and tired of high taxes and ever-rising inflation;

small businessmen angry at excessive government regulations and federal red tape;

born-again Christians disturbed about sex on TV and in movies;

parents opposed to forced busing;

supporters of the right to life and against federal financing of abortions;

middle class Americans tired of Big Government, Big Business, Big Labor and Big Education telling us what to do and what not to do;

pro-defense citizens alarmed by appeasement and weakness in U.S. foreign policy."

Mr. Viguerie has not detailed a new group; he has described the backbone of our country—those citizens who are pro-family, pro-moral, pro-life, and pro-American, who have integrity and believe in hard work, those who pledge allegiance to the flag and proudly sing our national anthem. He has described that group of citizens who love their country and are willing to sacrifice for her. America was built on faith in God, on integrity, and on hard work. Mr. Viguerie clearly names and points out the actions of those who have not been committed to these principles and have thus led to the weakening and the humiliation of a once great America.

It is now time for moral Americans to band together in a collective voice and make the difference in America by exerting an effort to make their feelings known. The godless minority of treacherous individuals who have been permitted to formulate national policy must now realize they do not represent the majority. They must be made to see that moral Americans are a powerful group who will no longer permit them to destroy our country with their godless, liberal philosophies.

The movement made up of conservative Americans can no longer be ignored and silenced. America's destiny awaits its action. Your children's future welfare will be decided by your present involvement.

Table of Contents

Introduction

Appendix

I

Why the New Right Is Winning

It's very simple.

The left is old and tired. The New Right is young and vigorous.

Most of the liberals' leaders of the past 30 years are gone — Adlai Stevenson, Walter Reuther, George Meany, Martin Luther King, Jr., Nelson Rockefeller, Hubert Humphrey, Robert Kennedy.

Our leaders are mostly in their 30's and 40's.

The liberals had a lot of victories over the last 50 years. But they've grown soft and sluggish.

We're lean and hungry — to gain victories for conservatism and to renew America.

There is a great yearning across America for a philosophy, for leaders, institutions and ideas that can help make America great again. Conservatives are answering that call.

Now, it is our turn, and we will seize this golden opportunity for the sake of our beloved nation, for all the people, including the liberals who have clearly lost confidence in themselves, and for generations yet unborn.

We conservatives have a vision about the future which I will try to describe in this book — along with the key role which the New Right, a group of dedicated men and women committed to freedom and opposed to tyranny, is playing and will continue to play.

We look forward, not backward, to the realization of the American dream, of each person reaching as high and as far as his ability and ambition will take him.

The liberals have not only lost confidence in themselves but in their ideas. We're convinced we have the ability to govern and *will* govern in the not-too-distant future.

The signs are everywhere.

Teddy Kennedy, the crown prince of liberalism, loses 40 out of 54 Democratic primaries and caucuses to Jimmy Carter, whose Presidential popularity has dropped lower than Richard Nixon's immediately prior to Nixon's resignation.

Ronald Reagan wins the GOP presidential nomination going away.

Liberals who control Congress try desperately to pretend they're balancing the federal budget.

The United Nations, once called the "last best hope for peace" on earth, is described by the *New York Times* (in 1974) as an organization whose actions have "all but eliminated (it) as a serious force for good or evil."

Milton Friedman, a conservative economist, wins the Nobel Prize for economics and writes a book about free enterprise that is number one on the *New York Times* bestseller list for six weeks.

2

Proposition 13 and its legislative offspring multiply in state after state. In 1978 alone, various limits on taxes or government spending are on the ballot in 16 states and win in 12.

In that same year, eight of liberalism's "brightest and best" in the Senate go down to defeat. Those taking political hemlock are Republicans Ed Brooke of Massachusetts and Clifford Case of New Jersey and Democrats Tom McIntyre of New Hampshire, Richard Clark of Iowa, Wendell Anderson of Minnesota, Floyd Haskell of Colorado, Paul Hatfield of Montana and William Hathaway of Maine.

The Carter administration puts SALT II on the back burner because it knows Senate conservatives have the votes to stop it.

George Gallup discovers that 49% of the registered voters across the U.S. now identify themselves as "right of center." Only 29% say they are "left of center." Only 10% claim they are "middle of the road" while 12% have no opinion. In 1964, 37% described themselves as liberals, 34% as conservatives and 29% had no opinion.

Liberal economics in 1980 have produced double-digit inflation, double-digit interest rates, 8% unemployed and the worst recession since World War II.

In 1966, according to the U.S. Census Bureau, there were 28.5 million Americans at or below the poverty level. By 1980, despite over $100 billion of taxpayer money spent, 29 million Americans still live below the $6,700 official poverty income line.

Liberal foreign policies of appeasement, retreat and accommodation have resulted in the loss of Vietnam, Laos and Cambodia — Cuban troops in

3

a dozen African nations — bewilderment and uncertainty among our allies.

Across the world, an estimated 1.8 billion people live, not by their choice, under Communist slavery.

In Red China alone, according to Professor Richard Walker, a leading Sinologist, at least 32 million men, women and children have died under communism.

One-third of Cambodia — approximately 2 million people — have been killed since 1975 by that country's brutal Communist rulers.

The White House remains silent for months about Communist rulers murdering men, women and children in Cambodia, but immediately screams about a relative handful of political prisoners in anti-Communist Chile.

Liberal national defense policies have resulted in the United States, long the world's strongest military power, falling behind Soviet Russia in every major area of conventional and strategic weaponry.

The Russians have nearly 15,000 strategic defense weapons, we have 309. They have 3,736 strategic offensive weapons, we have 2,124. They have 594 major ships and submarines, we have 296. They spent over $160 billion on national defense in 1978, we less than $120 billion.

America's collapse around the world is painfully obvious to everyone.

We're made fools of by Iran, a fourth-rate power.

Soviet Russia invades Afghanistan, and we feebly react by stopping the future sale of wheat which they turn around and buy from Argentina.

American liberals turn our Panama Canal over to a Marxist dictator.

It's past time that you and I and every other American asked some cold hard questions.

Who lost Iran?

Who lost Afghanistan?

Who lost Vietnam, Laos and Cambodia?

Who crippled the FBI and the CIA?

Who sold the Russians computers and other sophisticated equipment which have been used to stamp out freedom?

Who is keeping our kids from praying in school?

Who lets hardened criminals out on the street to kill, rape and rob again before their victims are buried or out of the hospital?

Who encourages American women to feel they are failures if they want to be wives and mothers?

Who tears apart the family and the community by the forced busing of children over the strong protests of their parents?

Who says that America should do little if anything to help human beings who are daily being killed and beaten up by Marxist dictators?

The answer in every case is LIBERALS.*

But America is waking up to what the liberals have been doing to it.

To quote Michigan professor Stephen Tonsor, "New Deal liberals are as dead as a dodo. The only problem is they don't know it."

---

*I do not mean that all liberals are guilty of all the things listed in this chapter. But most liberals have supported most of the plans and programs which have created the mess at home and abroad which we now find ourselves in.

Some do. State senators in Massachusetts ordered teachers to lead their classes in a "group recitation of the pledge of allegiance."

Maynard Jackson, the liberal black mayor of Atlanta, fired sanitation workers who had struck for higher wages, declaring, "Before I take the city into a deficit financial position, elephants will roost in the trees."

Professor James C. Coleman, author of a massive report in the 1960's which tipped the scale in favor of busing, now flatly admits he was wrong: "It is not the case that school desegregation, as it has been carried out in American schools, generally brings achievement benefits to disadvantaged (black) children."

Yes, liberalism has left its ugly scars everywhere.

Since 1973 and the Supreme Court decision allowing abortions on demand, an estimated 8 million babies have been killed — legally.

In St. Louis, the notorious Pruitt-Igoe housing project, conceived as a model of social concern for the poor, degenerated into a ghetto. Buildings were vandalized, then abandoned, and finally demolished. The cost to the American taxpayer: over $90 million, according to *Barron's*.

Many Americans, including some black leaders, have seen the light.

Black managers from McDonald's hamburger chain lobbied Congress to abandon organized labor's position and support a special reduced wage for young people — a longtime conservative solution to reduce massive unemployment among black teenagers.

Margaret Bush Wilson, national chairman of the NAACP, stunned many of her old liberal allies in 1977 by adopting a pro-energy development policy similar to that of free market advocates in the oil industry. As Mrs. Wilson explained, without apology, "New jobs come from economic growth in the private sector . . . . Government alone cannot be viewed as providing the only answer."

Rufus McKinney, Washington vice president of the Southern California Gas Co. and a former Labor Department lawyer, has little patience with liberal proposals for a less energy-intensive economy: "I think what (they're) really saying is we should go back to the good old days of sweatshops and slave labor . . . No energy, no growth, let's all go back to hand labor."

Charles Evers, a black Mississippi politician whose brother Medgar was murdered during the civil rights turmoil of the 1960s, declares he hates welfare: "There should be adequate care for those who need it but I'll be damned if I want to work 25 hours a day seven days a week, and pay to take care of somebody else's baby. We need a law in this country. . . making mandatory that every father must take care of his children."

Liberal hypocrisy and double-standards abound on all sides.

Liberal politicians lost a war in Vietnam they wouldn't let America mobilize to win — and wasted 55,000 American lives and over $135 billion.

Liberal politicians in Congress and the Ford administration approved a Swine flu program in 1976 that left 4,000 people dead, paralyzed or otherwise injured. More than $3.5 billion in damages against the federal government and the American taxpayer have been sought through lawsuits.

Liberal politicians have added nearly $350 billion to our federal debt in the past 10 years through deficit spending. At present, the share of every man, woman and child in America is nearly $4,000 each.

Liberal politicians have given us what liberal economists said was impossible — soaring inflation and serious recession at the same time.

Liberals delight in denouncing the Watergate sins of Richard Nixon. But they look the other way and refuse to seriously investigate the many abuses of liberal administrations, including:

— The financial wheeling and dealing of LBJ protege Bobby Baker.

— The wiretapping of Martin Luther King, Jr. under John F. Kennedy.

— The State Department's vicious vendetta against its chief security officer Otto Otepka because he gave his frank opinion of a high Kennedy appointee to the Senate Internal Security Subcommittee.

— The incredible memo of Victor Reuther of the United Auto Workers, who urged Attorney General Robert Kennedy to use federal agencies, including the IRS, to silence conservative critics of the Kennedy administration, like Senators Barry Goldwater and Strom Thurmond and Dr. Fred Schwarz's Christian Anti-Communism Crusade.

— Koreagate.

When folksinger Joan Baez, a long-time liberal heroine, called for condemnation of Communist murder and terror in Vietnam and Cambodia following the war, she was ignored by many liberals, including Jane Fonda.

Liberals in the 1950's and 1960's fought for civil rights legislation, supposedly to forbid discrimination of any kind based on race, creed, color, sex or national origin. But now they fight to establish quotas, preferential treatment and other forms of discrimination based on race, creed, color, sex and national origin.

Liberals condemn vote stealing and machine brutality in smalltown elections in the South. But they say little about vote stealing and other political dirty tricks in New York, Chicago and other big cities.

Most liberals support abortion of innocent babies. But they oppose capital punishment for convicted murderers.

Liberals condemn the "guilt by association" tactics practiced by Sen. Joseph McCarthy in the 1950's. But many delight in smearing any conservative even remotely associated with the John Birch Society or Richard Nixon.

On July 30, 1980, House Speaker Tip O'Neill said the Republicans in Congress were controlled by John Birchers.

Liberals howl about the "obscene profits" of oil companies. But they are silent about the higher profits of TV networks sympathetic to their views. In 1978, according to *Fortune*, Mobil Corporation's final return on equity was 12.6%. Gulf's return was 10.7%. Exxon's was 14%. The same year, ABC Television had a return of 21.6%, CBS 21% and RCA (which owns NBC) 17.4%.

Liberals remain mum about the double standards of leading liberal news media. In 1977, the *New York Times* ran 219 and the *Washington Post* ran 194 stories, editorials, columns and letters about human rights in South Africa. But the same two papers ran only 34 and 10 stories, respectively, about the most shocking violation of human rights in our age — the Communist slaughter of one-third the population of Cambodia.

Liberals label conservatives the preachers of hate, but the facts seem to indicate the opposite.

Jane Fonda — not Phyllis Schlafly — called America "a war machine" and "a murderer . . . barbaric." Bella Abzug — not Congresswoman Marjorie Holt — branded America "imperialistic . . . power mad . . . a vehicle for murder and oppression." Andrew Young — not William F. Buckley, Jr. — termed our ally Great Britain "a police state."

Some liberals, it's clear, hate not only the supposed "sin" of conservatism, but they hate the sinner too.

Sixteen years ago, following Barry Goldwater's nomination as the Republican nominee for President, California Gov. Edmund G. (Pat) Brown, a liberal Democrat, said, "I smell the stench of Nazism. I hear the march of storm troopers." Senator Goldwater, whose Jewish grandfather emigrated from what was then Russian Poland, was revolted by such typically "liberal" language.

AFL-CIO head George Meany said: "(There is) a parallel between Senator Barry Goldwater and Adolph Hitler."

Eight years later, in 1972, during another Presidential campaign, liberal George McGovern called America's policies in Vietnam "the most barbaric and inhumane since Adolph Hitler."

His running mate, Sargent Shriver, brother-in-law of the late John F. Kennedy, contented himself with calling President Nixon "the greatest murderer in the world today."

In May 1980, Vice President Mondale described Nixon as "the most miserable man ever to occupy any public office" in America.

And in August 1980, Health and Human Services Secretary Patricia Harris attacked Ronald Reagan because he was endorsed for President by the KKK — although Reagan disavowed their support.

Is it any wonder that with such a record, with such contempt for basic decency and basic American traditions, liberalism is in decline as the dominant force in American politics?

I have often been asked, What is a conservative? To paraphrase the late Frank Meyer, in his classic work *What Is Conservatism?* a conservative believes in six basic things: (1) a moral order, based on God; (2) the individual as the center of political and social action; (3) limited government; (4) a free as contrasted to a planned society; (5) the Constitution of the United States, as originally conceived by the Founding Fathers; and (6) the recognition of Communism as an unchanging enemy of the Free World.

You know, I have to smile when I read or hear that it is we conservatives who want to take America back to the 19th or 18th century.

I ask you: What is more reactionary than Ralph Nader's proposal that the Federal government issue charters for all U.S. corporations? It's medieval to say that the right of a business to function should come from government.

I ask you: Who are the slave traders of the 1980's? Those who sell illegal drugs, marijuana, heroin, cocaine, angel dust, uppers and downers.

Who's keeping our youth on the streets, unemployed and easy prey for drug pushers? Liberals who insist that a 17-year-old with the equivalent of a 5th grade education be paid a minimum wage of $3.10 or more an hour. The most frequent result: the young man or woman becomes another statistic on the unemployment rolls.

And why does this 17-year-old have the equivalent of a 5th grade education? Because the National Education Association and similar liberal groups have insisted that it's more important to bus children 20 to 40 miles every day, do away with grades, not worry about discipline, and protect teachers from fitness tests than to teach pupils how to read, write and do arithmetic.

Union officials and their liberal allies have their own form of slavery. It's called the union shop. In 30 of our 50 states, you must pay union dues or their equivalent to get or keep a job. If you don't belong to a union in those states, union officials say you don't have any right to work. As far as I'm concerned, that's right out of the Middle Ages.

Fortunately, more than 70% of the American people, liberal as well as conservative, think that's very wrong, and there is a growing national movement, led by Reed Larson and the National Right to Work Committee, to guarantee the freedom to join or not to join a union in every state.

Frankly, it is not conservatives but liberals who oppose progress, who want to take us back to a past era of few automobiles, undeveloped land, insufficient energy, a gray gloomy world, in which there is always less and less for more and more.

Who will suffer the most in this liberal "utopia"? The middle and working class, and the poor.

I am not exaggerating. Remember liberals opposed the building of the Alaska oil pipeline. Liberals oppose drilling for oil off both our coasts. Liberals are leading the fight against nuclear power plants, coal strip mining and oil shale development. They are pushing energy alternatives, like solar energy, which is great but won't be available on a significant scale for at least 20 years.

Liberals remind me of a gang of Don Quixotes gone berserk, not only tilting at windmills but trying to build them everywhere too.

I'm constantly amazed by the gall of liberals who claim they are "for" jobs and for more income for the average person, but who have such contempt and even hatred for businesses, large and small, particularly profitable businesses.

That's like being for eggs but against chickens. Or for milk but against cows. Where do liberals think jobs come from?

Yes, it's really very simple. Liberalism is almost stone cold dead in American politics. And conservatism is ready, willing and able to take its place, because the New Right has made a profound difference in conservative effectiveness and capacity these last few years. That difference has been made possible by the emergence of dynamic, brilliant, determined young leaders in and out of Congress.

For example, the Heritage Foundation, headed by Ed Feulner, has given tough-minded conservatives in Congress an intellectual base for their battles.

The Conservative Caucus, led by Howard Phillips, has organized local leadership which in turn has mobilized grassroots sentiment and action.

The Committee for the Survival of a Free Congress, directed by Paul Weyrich, and the National Conservative Political Action Committee, headed by Terry Dolan, have offered technical expertise, training, and money to right-of-center candidates of both parties.

While these conservative organizations, among many others I will be discussing later, were working on the outside, conservatives were organizing inside Congress for the very first time.

In 1973, the Republican Study Committee was born in the House of Representatives followed by the Senate Steering Committee. Both groups, made up of conservative Congressmen and Senators, have proved invaluable in stopping much left-wing legislation, in Congressional rules fights, the protection of legislative minority rights, battles over nominations to regulatory and other agencies and a host of other legislative struggles.

The House Committee's director is Richard Dingman while the Senate group is directed by Margo Carlisle—two of the most astute conservatives on Capitol Hill in developing short-range tactics and long-range strategy for the movement.

Meanwhile, long-established groups such as the National Right to Work Committee have expanded rapidly. The Committee went from a modest supporter list of 25,000 in 1971 to over 1.5 million in 1980. Right to Work has been joined by groups focused on Right to Life, pro-gun organizations like Gun Owners of America and pro-family and religious groups.

Older conservative organizations such as the American Conservative Union have operated at full tilt with intensive lobbying operations, coast-to-coast TV programs and upbeat publications. Political action committees (PACs) such as the Conservative Victory Fund have hired full-time staffs rather than using volunteers as in the past.

In other words, conservatives have shown up to play political ball on time, fully-equipped, in the correct ball park and with a game plan for victory.

At the same time, conservative leaders, not just spokesmen, have emerged in Congress — dedicated, principled men like Senators Orrin Hatch of Utah, Paul Laxalt of Nevada, Jesse Helms of North Carolina, James McClure of Idaho, Gordon Humphrey of New Hampshire, Bill Armstrong of Colorado, Congressmen Philip Crane of Illinois, Mickey Edwards of Oklahoma, Robert Dornan of California, Larry McDonald of Georgia, Henry Hyde of Illinois, Newt Gingrich of Georgia, Jim Jeffries of Kansas, George Hansen of Idaho, Jerry Solomon of New York, and many others.

We are determined to achieve our goal of organizing the conservative middle-class majority in America. We are convinced that such a new American majority is an idea whose time is now.

How will we do it? By appealing to:

— hard-working citizens sick and tired of high taxes and ever-rising inflation.

— small businessmen angry at excessive government regulations and federal red tape.

— born-again Christians disturbed about sex on TV and in movies.

— parents opposed to forced busing.

— supporters of the right to life and against federal financing of abortions.

— middle class Americans tired of Big Government, Big Business, Big Labor and Big Education telling us what to do and what not to do.

— pro-defense citizens alarmed by appeasement and weakness in U.S. foreign policy.

— every one who is unwilling to accept the liberal line that America has had her day in the sun, and that we must all tighten our belt and do with less.

I don't believe that. I don't accept that. And I don't think you do either.

America is still the land of opportunity, of optimism, of progress. We are not a tired, burnt-out, over-the-hill people — unless we allow ourselves to be convinced we are.

We of the New Right invite every American to join our crusade not only to preserve but to extend freedom to every segment of our society, every corner of our land.

What do we on the New Right stand for?

We believe in God and the importance of the traditional family.

We believe the way to have peace is to be stronger than the country that wants to conquer us.

We believe in fiscal prudence and helping only those who cannot help themselves.

We believe in and hold dear the spiritual convictions and moral foundations which made and continue to make America great.

We are Christian and Jewish. We are Republican, Democratic and Independent. Our first commitment is to political principles, not political parties.

We are mostly middle and working class. We wear a blue as well as a white collar.

We care about the social and cultural index of this nation as well as the consumer price index.

We live and work on Main Street, not Wall Street. We're more at home on the front porch than in the boardroom.

We are aggressive, committed, confident.

We don't give a darn about yesterday's defeats. We're interested in tomorrow's victories.

II

From Houston to
New York to Washington

I'm frustrated on any day when I haven't done something significant to help our country. That's my goal when I get up in the morning and that's my goal when the sun sets, and then some.

There's so much that needs to be done—help start a political action committee, encourage a candidate to run, write letters that motivate people and raise funds, bring key conservatives together to plan an important campaign, explain the New Right to a reporter or columnist, expand freedom in every possible way.

I was born in Golden Acres, Texas, right outside Houston, on September 23, 1933. My parents, Arthur and Elizabeth (nee Stoufflet), were of Louisiana French descent and moved to Texas the day they were married in September 1929, just before the Great Depression.

While the Viguerie family had some money and a great deal of real estate in South Louisiana, they lost just about everything in the financial panic of the early 1920's. Mother still retains a little of her Cajun accent. She spoke only French until she started school.

Dad had no college education (Mother had one year of college), and he went to work for the Shell Oil Co. as a construction worker. He was determined he wouldn't stay in the fields and he didn't. He worked his way up to top management.

Our family was thrifty. No money was ever wasted. My mother worked in a paper mill during World War II, doing a man's work. I suspect she actually did the work of several men. I remember we had a couple of cows, and I sold milk to the neighbors to bring in a little extra money for the family.

Dad usually worked two jobs—the one with Shell and the other hauling sand and gravel in a second hand dump truck. We also had a vegetable garden and Mother and Dad canned vegetables for use during the winter. Of course Mother was keeping house and looking after me and my sister, Annette, so she had two jobs too.

My folks were old-fashioned, industrious people who believed in saving their money for a rainy day. They were conservative, but we didn't sit around the dinner table talking politics. They lived what they believed in, and that included God.

I went to public schools all my life except for 2/3 of a year at a Catholic school. I was a poor student in high school, but I was determined to attend college.

In January 1952, when I was 19, I went off to college—Texas A & I, in Kingsville, about 250 miles from Houston. I wanted to be an engineer.

Why? Well, I had read that engineers were making a lot of money in South America so I figured I would make some quick money down south and come back to Houston—and run for Congress.

But, I had problems with algebra, so my teachers and I agreed I wasn't cut out to be an engineer. Well, I had observed that many politicians were lawyers. So I switched to pre-law.

In college, my big political heroes were "the two Macs"—Douglas MacArthur and Joseph McCarthy. I was very angry over the firing of MacArthur, who wanted to win the Korean war and beat the Communists.

And I felt the same way about Joe —he was a fighter fighting Communism. So I became a fighter. Even when he was inaccurate, McCarthy articulated my concern about a very big problem. There *are* Communists in this world. They are not the ghosts of a few right-wingers' imaginations.

While at Texas A & I, I joined a fraternity, Kappa Sigma, and became president in my last year there. Many of my buddies were veterans of the Korean War. The school had a Southern Baptist atmosphere and I was comfortable there. But I wanted to be close to the political action.

So, I switched schools in January 1956 to the University of Houston where I got my BS in political science with a minor in economics.

College was always very important to me. I knew it could open doors. Each summer, from the time I was 17, I worked at the refinery where my Dad worked, sometimes as a laborer. I dug ditches. I worked the midnight shift and the swing shift from 4 p.m. to midnight too. It was hard, exhausting work. Those summers were a strong incentive to finish college.

Still convinced that law was the road for me into politics, I enrolled in the University of Houston Law School. After 1½ semesters and a lot of C's and D's, I woke up to the fact that I was not going to be a second Clarence Darrow.

So I decided to get my military obligation out of the way. I enlisted in the U.S. Army Reserve program in March 1957, serving six months of active duty as an enlisted man and committing myself to another 7½ years in the reserves. I was stationed at Fort Chaffee, Arkansas.

As you can see, I was not exactly burning up the track and setting records. I was what you would call a late bloomer.

But I always knew I was going to do things, important things, that would make a big difference in people's lives.

And I knew I would do them through politics. Whenever I could make it, I was down at Republican headquarters, volunteering my time, working with the senior party, or with the Young Republicans.

I worked for Dwight Eisenhower in 1952 and 1956; I became chairman of the Harris County (Houston) Young Republicans. But I was always a conservative first.

I remember one time I invited Jack Cox, a big name Texas Democrat and a solid conservative, to speak at our YR barbecue. Several people strongly criticized the choice of a speaker since he was not a partisan Republican. I was hurt and didn't understand their objections. We had a great turnout, hundreds of people, and Jack Cox made a stirring speech. Looking back on it, I see now I practiced coalition politics without realizing it.

About this time, I got a clerk's job in an oil company for $90 a week. I remember standing at the elevator one day and hearing somebody say that my boss's boss was making $150 a week. I refused to believe it. I didn't think anyone his age could make that much money. I certainly didn't think I would, and I didn't care. I had plenty of politics to keep me busy in my spare time.

In 1960, as you know, Lyndon Johnson ran for vice president on the Democratic ticket with John F. Kennedy. What you may not remember is that Johnson also ran for reelection to the U.S. Senate from Texas that same year.

Tough little John Tower challenged LBJ, and we thought we had a chance if Nixon carried Texas and if enough people were upset at Johnson for running for two offices at the same time. We came up with a little slogan: "Double Your Pleasure, Double Your Fun—Vote Against LBJ Twice."

I was named Harris County campaign chairman for Tower and we put up a good fight. I did all the usual things, distributed literature, set up meetings, got out the vote. I also helped write a one-page fund raising letter for Tower that worked pretty well. I was kind of intrigued by it.

During the campaign, I heard that a group of young conservatives were meeting up north in Connecticut to form a national conservative youth organization, but I didn't go. I wasn't invited.

John Tower did very well that November—receiving 41% of the vote. It was a great statewide showing for a Republican and a professor

23

of economics who had never run for statewide office before. When Tower won the special senatorial election for LBJ's old seat in early 1961, I was not heavily involved.

After Tower was elected, I wanted to come to Washington with him in the worst way— as a mail room boy, as anything. I just knew that if I ever got the chance, good things would happen.

At last, in the summer of 1961, the opportunity came. And I did not hesitate. I guess you could say I got my break through a classified ad in *National Review*.

The ad said that a national conservative organization was looking for four field men. I checked it out with my friend David Franke, then with *National Review*, who told me the organization was Americans for Constitutional Action (ACA), an old-line conservative group founded in 1958. I was definitely interested.

I took a plane from Houston at midnight to save money and arrived in New York City at 4 a.m. I was as green as any kid who ever hit New York. I stood there at the east-side terminal with my suitcase. I was looking for a bus or cab to get to Dave Franke's apartment in Greenwich Village when I noticed these signs, "No Standing."

I wasn't 100% sure, but I didn't want to take any chances so I kept walking for blocks and blocks with the suitcase until I finally found Dave's apartment.

Later that morning I went uptown to *National Review*. I was about to cross East 35th Street when a man in a vested suit wearing a bowler hat and carrying an umbrella stopped me and said, "Mr. Viguerie, I presume?"

It was Bill Rusher, who took me inside the National Review building for the interview which turned out to be not for a field position with ACA but for executive secretary of Young Americans for Freedom (YAF), the conservative youth organization to whose founding I had not been invited because none of the organizers had any reason to know who Richard Viguerie was.

Actually, the job was to be Marvin Liebman's account executive for the YAF account. It was up to the YAF board of directors to hire the executive secretary.

I hit it off well with everyone I met, especially Marvin Liebman, who was to teach me so much about direct mail. I went back to Houston the next day to wait, but not for very long. A call soon came that I was hired.

I had been dating a beautiful young lady, Elaine O'Leary, for six months. We decided to get engaged right away—at the San Jacinto Monument outside Houston, where Texas won its independence. A few weeks later, I was back in New York City.

I was surprised to learn after arriving on the job that YAF, not one year old, was $20,000 in debt with only a couple of weeks operating money in the bank. Having just received my big break in life, I wasn't about to have it disappear on me. I was determined that YAF would succeed.

Marvin suggested I call on various wealthy contributors and ask them for money. My first visit was to Gov. Charles Edison, youngest son of the great inventor Thomas Edison and former Secretary of the Navy and Governor of New Jersey.

I have rarely met a more charming, gracious generous man. After making me feel comfortable (which was no small task), he wrote out a check for $500. YAF was to receive many more large checks from Governor Edison before he died in 1969.

Later I called on or visited Captain Eddie Rickenbacker, J. Howard Pew and others. I was reasonably successful in persuading them to make sizeable contributions to YAF.

But I'm basically a pretty shy person and I did not feel comfortable asking for money directly. So I began writing letters instead, and they seemed to work. So I wrote more and more letters and before many months, direct mail was my whole focus—for fundraising, subscriptions for *The New Guard*, YAF membership, everything.

In November 1962, YAF moved to Washington, D.C., and Elaine and I moved with them. (Elaine and I were married in Houston in February 1962.) In early 1963, I asked the YAF board to hire David Jones, the Florida state YAF chairman, to be the executive director and let me concentrate exclusively on direct mail.

I did this until December 1964 when I decided to start my own direct mail company. By this time Elaine and I had a two-year old daughter, Renée and a year-old daughter, Michelle. We had saved $4000. I took $400 from our savings and started the Richard A. Viguerie Company in January 1965.

At the beginning, I had one employee and 12,500 names of contributors. We located on Capitol Hill, three blocks from Congress.

How did I get those contributor names? Simple. After November 1964, I went down to the office of the Clerk of the House of Representatives. They had on file—as required by law—the names and addresses of all those who had given $50 or more to the Goldwater campaign.

I copied down their names and addresses by hand until my fingers were numb. It was legal to copy such public records, and to use the names for advertising, but no photo-copying was allowed. After a couple of weeks, I hired several women to do the copying. We wound up with 12,500 conservative contributors—the beginning of my famous list, without which I wouldn't be in business today.

I do not recommend what I did then as the best way to start a new business. YAF was my only major client and within a few months I lost it. But other business soon came along.

Our first big political client was Sen. Robert Griffin of Michigan, who ran for a full term to the U. S. Senate in 1966. We wrote some very successful letters. It was like fireworks going off. I was surprised, and I still am surprised by what happens in this business. It's what makes it so exciting.

Gradually as the company developed and I learned more and more about direct mail, I began to understand my role in the conservative movement.

There were different routes I could have gone. We had outstanding writers, debaters and public speakers like Bill Buckley, Bill Rusher, Russell Kirk. I could have tried to go that route. And I probably wouldn't have amounted to a hill of beans. I didn't have the educational background, and I was starting too late to catch up with the others who had a 20-year head start.

But I realized that what we didn't have was someone who could take the ideas, the writings and the books and market them to the people.

When a new cause came along or a new candidate or a new organization, we didn't really have someone who understood how to market them on a national scale.

So I set out to become the best marketer I could be. I determined to learn how to successfully market ideas to millions. But it's not easy to learn a new profession at 30 years of age.

It was particularly hard for my wife, Elaine, in the early years. She not only took care of our two small children, but she handled most all the duties normally handled by the husband, such as repairs to the house and car, yard work, paying bills, etc.

This allowed me to spend 3—5 hours a day reading and studying direct mail in addition to holding down a full time job.

Also no one ever went to college to be a direct mail expert. In fact, most all direct mail executives that I know got into the business accidentally.

My first direct mail teacher was Marvin Liebman, who was during the 1950's and through the mid-60's the principal public relations, fund raising and direct mail expert for the conservative movement. Then he decided to move to London to try his hand at his first love —producing plays.

My next teacher was one of the great men of direct marketing, Edward N. Mayer, Jr. I first met Ed in May 1965 when I attended a direct mail seminar he was conducting. And for the next 11 years (until he passed away) he was my teacher and friend.

Occasionally someone will ask me what I attribute my direct mail success to. I'm sure there are a number of factors, but one of the most important is working long hours. Included in my 12-hour days, Monday through Friday (plus 10 hours on weekends) are 3 hours a day reading and studying direct mail. I only know a few people in political direct mail (with the exception of Viguerie Co. employees, of course) who have read more than three or four books on direct marketing.

And back in the 1960's, most politicians did not understand direct mail at all. However, I knew one liberal politician who definitely appreciated its importance. George McGovern called me in 1967 to ask if I would like to help with the direct mail fund-raising for his 1968 Senate race.

I explained to the Senator that we were poles apart ideologically and he'd want someone more akin with his philosophy. We had a good long chat. It was clear he had an appreciation of the power of direct mail.

In 1969-70, after his reelection, McGovern told liberal organizations and candidates he wanted to help them raise money. He was generous. He signed a lot of fund-raising letters. He wanted only one thing—the names and addresses of people who responded to those mailings.

So in January 1971, when George McGovern announced for President he had a tremendous head start—a mailing list of thousands of people who had responded to an appeal for contributions for liberal causes—primarily to end the Vietnam War.

In 1967, instead of McGovern, I became involved with Max Rafferty, who beat U.S. Sen.

Tommy Kuchel, the Republican minority whip, in the June 1968 GOP primary in California. It was a big upset, a phenomenal event. I feel it was done largely with direct mail.

We mailed twice to 2 million Republican households in California. I'm confident that the over 5 million letters we mailed to people in California was the major reason a relatively unknown state superintendent of education with little campaign money was able to beat one of California's best known and most powerful politicians by 67,000 votes.

In the November general election, they asked us to mail only to the 60,000 previous Rafferty contributors and used the money mostly to buy TV ads. They didn't want a big direct mail effort. While that wasn't the only reason Rafferty lost badly in November, I think it certainly was one of the principal reasons.

Because of this experience and others in which we raised a lot of money for causes or candidates who would spend the money in what I viewed as an ineffective way, I began to insist, starting around 1974-75, that the money we raised through direct mail to voters in the candidates' district or state. The results have been good for the candidates and for the conservative movement.

Consider Phil Crane when he first ran for Congress from Illinois in a 1969 special election. He was one of 13 Republican primary candidates. If he won the primary, he would win the general because it was an overwhelmingly Republican district.

TV and newspaper advertising made little sense. His district was one of 14 districts covered by the Chicago mass media. Therefore, Phil needed to reach less than 5% of Chicago area citizens, the Republican voters in his district. Direct mail was the obvious medium to reach them.

We mailed two voter letters to every Republican in the district, and Phil Crane won in an upset. Just ten years later, Phil ran for the Republican nomination for President. He didn't win it but mark my words—he'll be back.

In 1971, I talked seriously to officials of the Committee to Re-Elect the President (CREEP). At the last minute we were denied the fundraising account. Then they came back to us in late 1971 about doing Nixon voter mailings. But Kissinger had already gone to Peking and the Nixon administration was busy "tilting" toward Red China and leaning away from our old friend and ally, Taiwan.

In addition, Nixon had established wage and price controls and announced that he was a Keynesian in economics, was pushing to enlarge the welfare programs and in general appeared to be trying to impress the *Washington Post* and the *New York Times* editorial page writers with how modern and progressive he was.

I decided I wanted no part of Nixon.

Reflecting on it, I realize that Nixon may never have had any deep-rooted beliefs or goals, except those that furthered his particular personal ambition.

I remember in the 1968 campaign that Nixon came out strongly about the weapons imbalance between us and the Soviets. But when Humphrey charged hard in the very last days of the campaign, Nixon panicked and reversed a previous statement on the weapons issue. It hit

31

me like a bolt of lightning. I said to myself, "That sonovagun really is sincerely, honestly tricky."

Because Nixon had moved to the left, I did the fund-raising for Congressman John Ashbrook of Ohio when he ran against Nixon in 1972 for the Republican presidential nomination. I lost $250,000 on the Ashbrook campaign, which did not turn out to be a serious effort. There wasn't even a campaign manager after the Florida primary in March although I lobbied hard for one. I saw clearly then that the people who were "leading" the conservative movement didn't understand how to lead.

I felt isolated and frustrated. I kept looking for people who could lead, who could make things happen. Finally, reluctantly, I began to call my own meetings.

I hosted one in December 1973 because I felt we were getting killed by Watergate. About 15 conservative Republican Congressmen attended a strictly private meeting. There was lots of talk, lots of suggestions, lots of smoke, but no fire. Nothing happened. They were afraid to act. They were impotent.

But as my wife Elaine likes to say, "When the good Lord closes a door he opens a window."

And who should come through the window and into my office in 1973, but the brother of George Wallace, who asked us to help the Governor retire his 1972 Presidential campaign debt.

We had doubts. They had reservations. Wallace was a Democrat and I was a Republican from that terrible place, Washington, D.C.

There were philosophical differences. Wallace was not a 100% conservative. He had a lot of populist, non-conservative ideas. But he and I agreed on about 80% of the important issues, social issues like busing and law and order, and the need for a strong national defense. So we struck a bargain.

I got a lot of criticism from old line conservatives. I was working for a prominent national Democrat—and national conservatives (until then) just didn't do things like that. Their negative reaction added to my growing disillusion with much of the established conservative leadership.

My working for Wallace—although I don't think I realized it at the time—was the beginning of my thinking in terms of coalition politics. I was encouraged by the fact that other conservatives like Paul Weyrich and Jeffrey St. John, the author and TV-radio commentator, were meeting and talking with Wallace. The three of us and our wives took a trip to Alabama to attend a social event at the Governor's Mansion in 1975. We were warmly received.

George Wallace was the first national candidate since Goldwater in 1964 that many conservatives strongly backed. We raised about $7 million for the Governor from 1973 through 1976. But I have to say that he disappointed me in that he never showed any interest in building a conservative movement.

Our efforts for Wallace were helped, believe it or not, by George McGovern, who had proven conclusively with his 1972 presidential race the power of direct mail. In fact, the person who suggested to the Wallace campaign that I be hired was Morris Dees, who did McGovern's direct mail in 1972, Carter's in 1976 and Kennedy's in 1980.

Another key factor in our growth was Watergate, which produced the Federal Election Campaign Act of 1974, limiting personal contributions to $1,000, per candidate per election.

Instead of turning to multi-millionaires like W. Clement Stone as Nixon did in 1972, presidential and all other federal candidates had to turn to the people. And there is no better way to get your message to the people and at the same time get them to give money than through direct mail.

I don't want to leave you with the impression that all of my clients are political candidates. Actually, less than 15% are. Many of our clients are what I call health and welfare clients.

But most are organizations with a conservative or right of center appeal. Our clients are concerned with issues such as gun control, pro-life, prayer in school, abuses by national union officials, wasteful government spending, high taxes, immorality on TV and in the movies, an educational system that can't educate, national defense and many other issues.

At the same time I'm proud of having helped elect fine conservatives like Jesse Helms, Strom Thurmond, Jim McClure, Orrin Hatch, Phil Crane, Mickey Edwards, Larry McDonald, Bob Livingston, Phil Gramm and Bob Dornan as well as helping effective conservative organizations like the National Right to Work Legal Defense Foundation, the National Rifle Association, *Human Events*, the American Security Council, The Conservative Caucus, the National Conservative Political Action Committee and dozens of others.

At present we have 250 employees, spread between The Viguerie Co. (including our multi-million dollar computer installation), our mailing company, a list company and a communications company which publishes *Conservative Digest*, a monthly magazine for the New Majority, edited by John Lofton, one of the conservative movement's most talented writers, and *The New Right Report*, a twice a month newsletter, written by James Martin, one of the conservative movement's foremost direct mail advertising experts. In the summer of 1982, we plan to move into our own 100,000 square foot building in Northern Virginia.

It has not been an easy path. I'm usually at my desk by 7 a.m., Monday through Saturday. I usually eat my lunch at my desk or skip lunch. I bring home 10 to 12 hours of work on the weekends. This pace is less than it used to be, but I am always aware of what Winston Churchill once said: "So much to be done and so little time in which to do it."

I am deeply indebted to the employees of The Viguerie Company who make it possible for me to devote so much of my time and energy to the New Right.

They work long and hard and selflessly. Many times when I leave the office at 7 or 8 p.m., I'll pass 5 or 6 people who will be working on a mailing whose deadline is fast approaching. A lot of people spend a lot of time making sure that deadlines are met.

My success, such as it is, is not mine alone but a success based on the talent, experience and professionalism of hundreds of dedicated men and women, from executive vice president to file clerks.

By 1974 The Viguerie Co. was successful and well established. Elaine and I and our three children—Renée, Michelle and Ryan—lived in a very comfortable home in Bethesda, Maryland. I should have been satisfied. I had come a very long way from the Houston oil refinery, a walk-up flat in Greenwich Village and a three-room office over Morton's Pharmacy on Capitol Hill.

But I knew I would never be happy until other conservatives and I came together and truly began saving our nation and the world from the liberal leaders and the liberal ideas which had almost destroyed us.

And so in 1973 and 1974, I began making new friends or reestablishing acquaintances with individuals who shared my concern and my frustration—people like Paul Weyrich, Morton Blackwell, Charlie Black, Howard Phillips, Bill Richardson, Woody Jenkins and others. We discovered that we all brought new things to the table.

Howard's idea was to go to the grassroots. Paul stressed precinct organization. Morton was my eyes and ears to the conservative movement, always insisting we pay attention to studying how to win and to the training of young people. Woody was a Louisiana Democrat who kept saying that not *all* the good guys were in the Republican Party.

Slowly but surely we came together. I'll never forget Morton telling me how shocked he was when he arrived in Washington as executive director of the College Republicans in the Sixties and discovered that Barry Goldwater, Strom Thurmond and John Tower didn't sit down each week to plan the conservative strategy for that week.

But without the battles which they won and lost, and those of many other conservatives in and out of Congress, we would have been forced to start almost from scratch. Instead, a solid foundation for the conservative movement had been built by solid men and women in the 1950's and 1960's.

III

The Foundations of the New Right

Two men are more responsible than any other for the strength and vitality of conservatism in America today — Bill Buckley and Barry Goldwater.

Without them, an effective conservative movement might never have begun.

William F. Buckley, Jr., has played so many roles it's hard to name them all: Editor of *National Review*, the conservative intellectual journal for 25 years. Syndicated columnist since 1962 whose witty commentary has kept liberals off balance year after year. Host of the weekly TV program *Firing Line* since 1966, the only regular conservative show on the nation's most important mass medium. Author of a dozen-plus best-selling books, both fiction and non-fiction.

God and Man at Yale was published almost 30 years ago, in 1951. It was a literary shot heard around the nation, if not the world. And Bill has written so many other important books since then, not the least being his novels about a CIA agent named Blackford Oakes.

I ask you: Who else but Bill Buckley could write three best-selling books favorable to the CIA when that agency, unfortunately, has a reputation lower than a snake's belly?

Less well known, I'm sure, have been Bill Buckley's many organizational contributions to the conservative movement. Young Americans for Freedom was founded at his family's Sharon, Conn., home in 1960. Bill was instrumental in helping to organize in 1961-62 the Conservative Party of New York, which has played such a decisive role in electing dozens of conservatives to the state legislature and the U.S. Congress.

Bill Buckley himself ran for mayor of New York City in 1965 in a memorable campaign. His effort is probably best remembered for his wisecrack response when he was asked what he would do if he won: "Demand a recount."

But in fact, in that race and elsewhere he proposed a number of sensible programs, prompting him to later write a small but important book, *Four Reforms*, which touched on welfare, taxes, crime and education.

Bill was a major figure in the 1964 founding of the American Conservative Union, which alone carried much of the organizational burden of the right until the mid-70's when New Right groups like The Conservative Caucus, the Committee for the Survival of a Free Congress and the National Conservative Political Action Committee were formed. He also worked closely with a number of anti-communist organizations in the 1950's and 1960's, including probably the best known of all—the Committee of One Million (Against the Admission of Communist China to the United Nations).

Through his wit, intelligence, and willingness to stand up for conservative principles, Bill Buckley, almost single-handedly, made the word "conservative" respectable and accepted.

Young people in today's climate may not believe it, but in the mid-1950's when Bill Buckley started *National Review*, you did not shout your conservatism from the roof tops—you whispered it behind closed doors.

Particularly through *National Review*, he has helped develop some of our finest young conservative writers and thinkers—people like George Will, Joseph Sobran, George Nash, Neal Freeman, Richard Brookhiser and others.

It was Bill Buckley's unique contribution to draw together, basically through *National Review*, three kinds of conservatives in America. As outlined by George Nash in his definitive book, *The Conservative Intellectual Movement in America*, they were:

● The "classical liberals" or libertarians, who resisted the threat of government to liberty, free enterprise and the individual, including men like Frank Chodorov and John Chamberlain.

● The "new conservatives" or traditionalists, who urged a return to traditional religious and ethical standards, including men like Russell Kirk and Richard Weaver.

● The militant anti-communists, who believed that the West was engaged in a deadly struggle with communism, including men like Whittaker Chambers and James Burnham.

The New Right owes much of what we believe in and are fighting for to such outstanding men and the catalyst who brought them together, William F. Buckley, Jr.

Our debt to Barry Goldwater is as great. The Presidential campaign of 1964 was the first major political experience for most of us in the New Right.

As Paul Weyrich says, "Even if we did nothing but wear a Goldwater button or attend a rally—and some of the New Right are so young that is all they did—that campaign left an indelible mark on us."

You may remember some of the things Barry Goldwater said in his campaign—honest, true, blunt things. His words came back to haunt Americans in the aftermath of Vietnam, Agnew, Watergate, Nixon, and Carter.

Goldwater said in his 1964 campaign:

"There is violence in our streets, corruption in our highest offices, aimlessness among our youth, anxiety among our elders. . .

"Where examples of morality should be set, the opposite is seen. Small men, seeking great wealth or power, have too often and too long turned even the highest levels of public service into mere personal opportunity."

And he said:

"We have got to stop inventing ways to spend money and start thinking of ways to save some!

"Our growing revenue potential must be used to reduce taxes, eliminate perpetual deficits and repay debt, not to finance wasteful government spending or give the Administration in power even more power for political manipulation."

And he said:

"We (must) brand Communism as the

principal disturber of peace in the world today — indeed, the only significant disturber of peace.

"We must make it clear that until its goals of conquest are absolutely renounced, and its relations with all nations tempered, Communism and the governments it now controls are enemies of every man on earth who is or wants to be free."

As Barry Goldwater said on January 3, 1964, when he announced his candidacy for the Republican nomination for President:

"I will offer a choice, not an echo."

27,174,898 Americans wanted that choice, and voted for the conservative Senator from Arizona on November 3, 1964.

Yes, it's true he lost badly, receiving only 39% of the vote and carrying only six states—Arizona and five Deep South states, Mississippi, Alabama, Louisiana, South Carolina and Georgia.

But it's also true that on the July day he was nominated, Senator Goldwater's own polls showed that only a little more than 20% of the electorate would vote for him. And as he writes in his autobiography, *With No Apologies*:

"In our public opinion samplings I was never more than 30 to Lyndon Johnson's 70 percent."

It was no small feat to double his poll position during a dirty campaign which included two TV commercials which pictured Barry Goldwater as a man who would bring nuclear death and destruction to the world.

Here is the *New York Times*' description of one TV spot: "A little girl licking an ice cream cone appeared on millions of television screens all over America. (A woman's voice) told her that people used to explode atomic bombs in the air and that the radioactive fallout made children die. The voice then told of a treaty preventing all but underground nuclear tests and how a man who wants to be President of the United States voted against it.

" 'His name is Barry Goldwater,' she said, 'so if he is elected, they might start testing all over again.' A crescendo of Geiger counter clicks almost drowned out the last words. Then came the male announcer's tag line: 'Vote for President Johnson on November 3rd. The stakes are too high for you to stay home.' "

And here is the *Times* report of the second TV commercial:

"A little girl with wind tossed hair was shown in a sunny field picking daisies. As she plucks the petals of one daisy, she counts. On the sound track, coming in stronger and stronger, a male voice counts backwards.

"When the girl reaches 10, the man's voice, in the doom-filled cadences of the countdown, reaches zero. The screen is rent by an atomic explosion.

" 'These are the stakes,' says the voice of Lyndon Baines Johnson. 'To make a world in which all of God's children can live, or go into the dark. We must either love each other, or we must die.'

"The doom-voice returns, urging viewers to vote for President Johnson on November 3rd: 'The stakes are too high for you to stay home.' "

It did not matter, as Senator Goldwater pointed out, that never once in any of his writings or his speeches did he advocate the use of military power to destroy Soviet Russia. What he did state repeatedly was that "the surest road to peace is through military strength."

Conservatives young and old learned a lot during the 1964 Presidential campaign. We learned how to stuff envelopes, ring doorbells, get out the vote on election day and contribute to a political campaign.

We also learned how to win a Presidential primary, how to select delegates to a national convention, how to put together a campaign team, how to use TV, radio and newspapers to communicate our message, how to go to the people at the grassroots for their help.

In fact, the Goldwater campaign of 1964 paved the way for the later successful use of direct mail by conservatives, especially the New Right.

For example, when Richard Nixon ran for President in 1960, individual financial contributors to his campaign ran between 40,000 and 50,000 people. In *The Conscience of a Majority*, Senator Goldwater wrote: "The best count ever made of the individual contributions to my [Presidential] campaign. . . put the total at around 661,500."

Barry Goldwater also showed that it was possible to reach out and attract conservatives from every party and every walk of life. He wrote eloquently about these Americans way back on January 11, 1961:

"There are literally scores of millions of Americans who are either outside the organized pressure groups or find themselves represented by organizations with whose policies they disagree in whole or in part.

"These millions are the *silent Americans* who, thus isolated, cannot find voice against the mammoth organizations which mercilessly pressure their own membership, the Congress, and society as a whole for objectives which these silent ones do not want. They, thereby, have become the 'forgotten Americans' despite the fact that they constitute the majority of our people."

Barry Goldwater spoke for these silent, forgotten Americans in his 1964 Presidential campaign and in his many speeches and books, especially one, *The Conscience of a Conservative*.

It is, simply, the most popular political book in American history. Published in March 1960 by Victor Publishing, a small conservative firm, it has sold more than 3 million hardback copies and many millions of paperback copies.

In just 134 pages, *The Conscience of a Conservative* outlines a basic program for the preservation and extension of freedom in America and around the world. Its proposals for achieving economic strength at home and military strength abroad make just as much sense today as they did 20 years ago.

Which comes as no surprise to any conservative. Some things never change—like man's spiritual nature, the danger of a too powerful central government, Communism's unchanging goal of wanting to bury us.

Barry Goldwater has been more than vindicated by the events of the 20 years since he wrote *The Conscience of a Conservative* and the 16 years since he ran for President of the United States. Conservatives owe him a debt which can never be adequately paid.

Although they have not played so prominent a role as Bill Buckley and Barry Goldwater, there are others who deserve to be mentioned for their important early contributions to the conservative movement.

• Frank Hanighen in 1944 founded *Human Events*, then a weekly newsletter, now a newspaper, which has consistently told conservatives what is really happening in Washington. Today, Tom Winter and Allan Ryskind continue to publish one of the best political newspapers in the country.

• In 1953, Russell Kirk wrote the classic book, *The Conservative Mind*, which provided a solid philosophical base for American conservatism.

• The same year, Frank Chodorov started the Intercollegiate Society of Individualists, now the Intercollegiate Studies Institute (ISI). Under the leadership of Victor Milione for the past 22 years, ISI has given conservative students books, seminars, publications and a sense of not being the only conservative in the world.

• Sen. Strom Thurmond of South Carolina has been a star in the conservative firmament for more than 30 years, contributing his time and talent again and again.

• Frank Meyer, author and senior editor of *National Review*, spent most of his life trying to "fuse" together the libertarian and traditionalist strains of the conservative movement. He was not only a writer but a doer, declaring that brave words without equally brave action meant very little.

• Ronald Reagan, as governor of California and three-time candidate for the Presidency, has put conservative principles into action. He played a key role in the continuing development of Young Americans for Freedom in the 1960's and 1970's and in 1977 formed one of the largest conservative PACs in the country — Citizens for the Republic.

• Whittaker Chambers alerted countless Americans to the epic struggle between the Free World and communism through his moving book, *Witness*.

• Dr. Fred Schwarz of the Christian Anti-Communism Crusade put it as simply and persuasively as is possible with his classic work, *You Can Trust the Communists — To Be Communists*.

• Brent Bozell, as editor of the Catholic magazine, *Triumph*, and collaborator with Barry Goldwater on *The Conscience of a Conservative*, was one of the first conservatives to warn of the dangers of relying exclusively on the Republican Party.

• Milton Friedman spoke, wrote about and promoted conservative economics so brilliantly that they finally had to give him a Nobel Prize.

• Walter H. Judd, a former Congressman, medical missionary and staunch anti-communist, was the driving force behind one of the very first conservative single issue groups — The Committee of One Million, launched in 1953.

• John Fisher founded the American Security Council in 1955 and has built it into the most active pro-national defense organization in the country, never hesitating to use the latest technological developments.

• M. Stanton Evans, as author of YAF's Sharon Statement, newspaper editor, TV and radio commentator, former chairman of the

American Conservative Union and now head of the ACU Education and Research Institute and its Washington Journalism Center, has been a major architect of American conservatism.

These are just some of the dedicated conservatives who helped lay the foundation for one of the most dramatic developments in modern American politics — the birth of the New Right.

By the early 1970's, many of us (Paul Weyrich, Howard Phillips, Morton Blackwell, and others) were working in the Nation's Capital. We met informally from time to time, at a luncheon or at a social function, to talk conservative politics. Occasionally, we worked together to help a rising conservative — like Congressman Jim McClure when he ran for and won a Senate seat from Idaho in 1972.

But there was no organized, continuing effort to exert political influence on elections, on Capitol Hill, on the news media and on the nation at large.

It was almost as though we were waiting for a challenge which would force us to test our strength and our convictions. And one day, something did happen which so angered us that we resolved to fight back as hard as we knew how. We haven't stopped fighting since.

IV

The Birth of the New Right

One morning in August 1974, I turned on my television to watch our brand-new President Gerald Ford announce he was picking Nelson Rockefeller to be his vice president.

Nelson Rockefeller! The liberal who attacked Barry Goldwater during the GOP primaries in 1964 so strongly it helped defeat Goldwater in November. The liberal who got Richard Nixon to agree to the infamous midnight Pact of Fifth Avenue in 1960, placing a liberal stamp on the GOP platform. Nelson Rockefeller—the high-flying, wild-spending leader of the Eastern Liberal Establishment.

As a conservative Republican, I could hardly have been more upset if Ford had selected Teddy Kennedy.

After all, there were a number of good conservatives Ford could have picked, starting with Ronald Reagan and Barry Goldwater. But Jerry Ford revealed the true colors of so-called "moderate" Republicanism by choosing the very symbol of everything we conservatives had always opposed.

I immediately got on the phone and invited about 14 conservative friends to dinner the next night to talk about how we could stop Rockefeller from becoming vice president.

We were an assortment of political activists, Capitol Hill aides, journalists, a lawyer or two, leading Washington conservatives. We came up with a few good ideas, but I soon realized the conservatives didn't have the leadership or the clout to stop Nelson Rockefeller from becoming the next vice president. And we quickly learned that most Republicans, while not enthusiastic about Rockefeller and even preferring Reagan or Goldwater, had no stomach for a hard-nosed fight so soon after Richard Nixon's resignation.

As they had so often in the past, most Republicans chose to put party before principle.

Well, we didn't stop Rocky. And I realized that we might be close to losing the entire battle to the left unless some of us who had not previously taken a leadership role stepped out front and center. That night in August it became clear to me that the conservatives were in desperate need of leadership.

I decided to give up some of the time I was spending with my family, on golf, vacations, etc., and spend that time helping to organize the movement. In short, I decided to stop following and start doing some leading of my own.

There were, of course, other factors beside the Rockefeller nomination which brought us together.

Some of us, like Howard Phillips, had been an important part of the Nixon administration. Howard had waged a three-year campaign to secure permission from the Nixon administration to abolish the Office of Economic Opportunity (OEO), and its programs.

Buoyed by the promise of a Nixon veto of any OEO funding after June 30, 1973, he set out to do just that. Then as Richard Nixon became more and more preoccupied with Watergate, liberal White House staffers decided OEO dismantlement was too controversial. They decided instead to continue and even expand OEO programs.

In mid-1974, Howard and I started Conservatives for the Removal of the President—CREEP II. We were afraid Nixon would make concessions to the Russians as he tried to deal with Watergate. I had known Howard from the early days of YAF and admired his energy, brains and determination.

Others had been disillusioned by Spiro Agnew's fall. Conservatives had applauded Agnew's attacks on liberal hypocrisy and elitism in the news media and elsewhere. They felt Agnew had given voice to the Silent Majority. But he turned out to be all too willing to compromise himself and his office for a few dollars and some groceries.

Others of us were tired of losing. The old right many times gave the appearance they believed that being right was enough—regardless of the battle's outcome. Also, because they had been fighting liberalism since the 1930's, older conservatives tended to be defensive and defeatist. They spent so much time putting out liberal fires, they had little time to start any fires of their own.

Others of us were just plain impatient. These young conservatives were ambitious, aggressive, coming into their prime. They had had enough of sitting around and waiting for older conservatives to start leading.

I would have preferred then as now to have stayed home with my wife and children, be on the golf course and/or be in my office tending to my direct mail business, but there was work to be done.

And I think that most of my associates in the conservative movement would also prefer to be home with their families rather than in early morning and late night meetings, airports, hotel rooms, making speeches to strangers, living out of a suitcase, etc.

Why have we taken up the challenge? Because there are people dying and suffering at the hands of brutal dictators. There are people who are slaves to drugs, or without jobs, or not eating, or going out of business, and in numbers never dreamed of before, all because of government failures and interference.

The liberals and the socialists have had their opportunity to try and help people. But ironically, almost all the problems in the world have gotten much worse since the liberals took control of the world's most influential and powerful nations.

Basically, we on the New Right had four things in common:

1. A developing technical ability—in direct mail, in mass media, in practical politics.

2. A willingness to work together for the common good.

3. A commitment to put philosophy before political party.

4. An optimism and a conviction that we had the ability to win and to lead America.

We didn't call ourselves the New Right, at least not right away. The term was first used but in a different context by Lee Edwards in 1962 when he proposed a conservative platform for Young Americans for Freedom in an article in *The New Guard*. The article was entitled: "The New Right: Its Face and Future."

Conservative columnist M. Stanton Evans used the phrase in 1969 to describe the emerging conservatism on college campuses—contrasting the New Right with the New Left then getting so much publicity.

But political columnist and analyst Kevin Phillips was the first, in 1975, to use the term in talking about "social conservatives" and the first to use it in regard to the collective efforts of Paul Weyrich, Howard Phillips, Terry Dolan, myself and others.

The more we talked and worked and planned together, the more we realized we could make things, important things, happen. We learned together and we helped educate each other about movement building. And the man perhaps with the broadest vision was Paul Weyrich. I can think of no one who better symbolizes or is more important to the conservative movement than Paul Weyrich.

He started or played the critical role in such key conservative groups as the Heritage Foundation, the American Legislative Exchange Council, the Republican Study Committee, the Senate Steering Committee, Library Court, to name but a few. He and Howard Phillips spent countless hours with electronic ministers like Jerry Falwell, Jim Robison and Pat Robertson, urging them to get involved in conservative politics.

Many influential people are involved in major conservative activities because Paul recognized their potential and sought them out. He has probably spent several thousand hours in one-on-one meetings, urging influential people to get involved.

Paul's success is based on three things: (1) His absolute integrity—he is totally dedicated to conservative principles, (2) His absolute reliability. If he makes a commitment, he holds to it, no matter what, and (3) His brain. Paul is one of the most intelligent and perceptive people I have ever met.

Paul remembers the day he decided to switch from supporting conservative leaders to becoming one himself. He had been working as an aide to Sen. Gordon Allott of Colorado, a solid Republican conservative, for several years.

One day, during the first Nixon administration, he sat in on a meeting of top liberals planning to push through enactment of an open housing bill. Present were a high White House official (appointed by Nixon but a certified liberal), a columnist for a Washington newspaper, someone from the Brookings Institution, representatives from various black pressure groups and aides to a dozen key senators.

"They planned their campaign in a very impressive way," remembers Paul. The Senate aides committed their bosses to make statements and contact other Senators. The White

House official promised to keep track of the Administration's actions. The columnist said he would write a favorable article. The Brookings man promised to publish a study in time to affect the debate. The blacks agreed to provide street demonstrations at the right moment.

"I saw how easily it could be done," recalls Paul, "with planning and determination, and decided to try it myself." And he has, very successfully.

In 1974, with the financial help of business leader Joseph Coors and at my own strong urging, Paul Weyrich founded the Committee for the Survival of a Free Congress (CSFC). My company was more than willing to do the direct mail advertising. CSFC wasted no time in making a difference.

Less than four years later, in 1978, CSFC spent $400,000 to help elect 31 conservative candidates, including Senators Gordon Humphrey, Roger Jepsen of Iowa, Bill Armstrong of Colorado and John Warner of Virginia, as well as Congressmen Jim Jeffries of Kansas, Bill Carney of New York, Ken Kramer of Colorado, Jerry Solomon of New York and Wayne Grisham of California.

Other leading members of Congress that CSFC has helped elect are Senators Orrin Hatch of Utah and Malcolm Wallop of Wyoming and Congressmen Mickey Edwards of Oklahoma and Robert Dornan of California.

Paul preaches the gospel of organization, insisting that campaigns he supports be well-organized.

"In the past," he says, "many of our conservative candidates ran strictly issue-oriented campaigns but didn't adopt many of the technical operations necessary to win."

Paul is very high on the "Kasten Plan" (named after former Congressman Robert Kasten), by which a specific voter turnout goal is set for every precinct in the Congressional district and a precinct chairman is given the responsibility of meeting this goal.

CSFC sponsors week-long schools, covering all the elements of a campaign, including surveys, the media, opposition research, precinct organization, recruitment and coalition building. At the week's end, teams are pitted against each other in a simulated election.

"You really find out from the results who has learned from the school and who has not," he notes.

Paul looks for and supports candidates who have a winning attitude. "If a candidate comes in here and says, 'Well, I don't think I can win, but boy, I think I can run a good race,' he doesn't get our help. We want candidates who say, 'By golly, we can lick this guy, and here's how we're going to do it, and every waking moment of my life and that of my family is going to be spent toward that objective.' "

Paul typifies the political philosophy of the New Right which parallels the military philosophy of Douglas MacArthur, "There is no substitute for victory."

In fact, Paul likes to argue that we are at war. "It may not be with bullets," he concedes, "and it may not be with rockets and missiles, but it is a war nevertheless. It is a war of ideology, it's a war of ideas, it's a war about our way of life. And it has to be fought with the same intensity, I think, and dedication as you would fight a shooting war."

Paul is constantly looking for new groups to add to the growing New Right coalition—anti-abortion groups, veterans groups, religious groups, tax groups, small businessmen, etc. He believes that family-oriented issues will be the key issues of the 1980's. He is, for example, president of the Free Congress Research and Education Foundation, which has a Family Policy Division specializing in such issues.

He compares the New Right to the "brain trust" that came in with Franklin Delano Roosevelt when he was first elected in 1932 (11 years before Paul Weyrich was born).

"We are radicals," he says, "who want to change the existing power structure. We are not conservatives in the sense that conservative means accepting the status quo.

"We cannot accept the status quo. Today isn't the same as the 1950's when conservatives were trying to protect what was, Constitutionally, economically and morally, in the control of more or less conservative people."

Today's establishment, he declares, is in the hands of liberals who must be resisted and then replaced.

It is liberals who came up with giving away the Panama Canal, he argues.

It is liberals who have put us in a second rate military position through a failure to develop new weapons and via one-sided treaties like SALT I.

It is liberals who want to spend so much money that the future of our children is already mortgaged.

It is liberals who want the Federal government to intervene in nearly every aspect of our lives.

"We have to take a turn in the other direction," Paul asserts. "The New Right does not want to conserve, we want to change — we *are* the forces of change. And if people are sick and tired of things in this country, then they had best look to conservative leadership for that change."

To leaders, for instance, like 29-year-old John (Terry) Dolan, chairman of the National Conservative Political Action Committee (NCPAC). Founded in 1975 by young conservatives Charlie Black, Roger Stone and Terry Dolan, NCPAC has become the largest conservative PAC in the country. It has distributed $1.2 million just in cash and in-kind contributions to political races in its first five years. It has spent millions of dollars more in other areas, such as advertising, to elect conservatives. I'm proud to say that my company has handled the direct mail for NCPAC.

Terry himself helped engineer the revolutionary 1978 Senatorial campaign of Gordon Humphrey, which used Boston radio and TV for the first time in a major way to reach the New Hampshire voters. Under his guidance, NCPAC has made a specialty of participating in primaries, believing that a well-placed dollar in a primary campaign which is usually poorly organized and under-financed, has more clout than in a general election, when more money and organization are generally available.

NCPAC relies heavily on research and polling, a reflection of one of its founders, conservative pollster Arthur Finkelstein. The committee works not only in Federal but in state and local campaigns where again a modest amount of money or organization can make a big difference.

NCPAC has pioneered in what is called the "independent expenditure campaign"—in which a political action committee may legally spend as much as it wants for or against a candidate so long as there is no contact whatsoever between the PAC and the candidate and his organization.

For example, a PAC called Conservatives for Reagan could legally spend $5 million or whatever it could raise to help elect Ronald Reagan President as long as none of the PAC's leadership was in contact in any way with Reagan or his staff. Or the same PAC could spend millions attacking Jimmy Carter—again as long as it was not coordinating its efforts in any way with the Reagan campaign.

In 1978, NCPAC ran independent expenditure ads in Iowa, Colorado and Kentucky, attacking Senators Dick Clark, Floyd Haskell and Walter Huddleston for supporting the Panama Canal treaties—ads which contributed to the defeat of Clark and Haskell. This year, NCPAC is sponsoring independent expenditure advertising campaigns against six of the most liberal U.S. Senators—George McGovern of South Dakota, Frank Church of Idaho, John Culver of Iowa, Birch Bayh of Indiana, Thomas Eagleton of Missouri and Alan Cranston of California.

Here is just one anti-McGovern TV spot which will give you an idea of how NCPAC drives the liberals crazy:

"Globetrotter is a great name for a basketball team.

"But it's a terrible name for a senator.

"Only one Senator did more globetrotting last year than George McGovern.

"While the energy crisis was brewing, George McGovern was touring Cuba with Fidel Castro. He also took a one-month junket to Africa. All at taxpayer's expense."

Terry Dolan is busy on many different conservative battlegrounds. He is chairman of the Washington Legal Foundation, as well as Conservatives Against Liberal Legislation (CALL), a lobbying group.

What Paul Weyrich is to the conservative movement in Washington, D.C., 39-year-old Howard Phillips is to the grassroots movement around the country.

Howard is founder and national director of The Conservative Caucus, launched in 1975, which now has 300,000 contributors and supporters, chairmen in 250 Congressional districts and an annual budget of almost $3 million. Again, my company was happy to undertake the direct mail advertising program for the Caucus at the beginning and continuing to this day.

The Conservative Caucus' basic goal is to mobilize a Congressman's constituents so as to influence his legislative record and thereby national policy.

"We have three basic jobs," Howard explains, "(1) to recruit and train local leaders, (2) to lobby at the grassroots level, and (3) to help set the agenda for national debate, by emphasizing the conservative viewpoint on key issues like the Panama Canal, SALT II and Communism in Central America.

"I firmly believe that right now, if we fight only at the national level, we lose. But using our strength at the local level, at the grassroots, we can win. And we have.

"If it had not been for the 50-state campaign of The Conservative Caucus and the SALT Syndrome film of the American Security Council, SALT II might have passed the U.S. Senate in the summer of 1979."

The Caucus' sister organization is The Conservative Caucus Research, Analysis and Education Foundation, a tax-deductible organization, which publishes *Congressional Report*, *Senate Report* and *Senate Roll Call*, maintains an active Speakers Bureau and a Legislative Data Bank.

Recently, The Foundation initiated a Research Bureau program to monitor federal departments and agencies. In 1979, it sponsored the Religious Roundtable, which has become a major educational force in briefing religious leaders on public policy issues.

"Conservatives," insists Howard, "must establish ourselves first as the opposition, then the alternative, finally the government."

The New Right, he says, was born out of Watergate.

"Many of us used to believe that conservative fortunes were synonymous with Republican fortunes. We placed an inordinate hope in the GOP and in Richard Nixon.

"Because many key GOP Congressmen and Senators were so personally fond of Richard Nixon, they frequently acquiesced in liberal policies, simply because Nixon was their advocate. Watergate changed that."

Another key leader is Morton Blackwell, described by *Human Events* as "the eyes and ears" of the New Right. Before joining Sen. Gordon Humphrey's staff in mid-1979 as policy director, Morton was chairman of the Committee for Responsible Youth Politics (CRYP), editor of *The New Right Report* and a key executive of my company for 7 years. He is a contributing editor to *Conservative Digest*, organizer of an informal bi-weekly luncheon meeting of conservative PAC leaders and president of the Leadership Institute, which trains young people in leadership techniques. At 40, he is a major figure in the New Right and liaison among the various elements of the Washington conservative community.

Through CRYP and the Leadership Institute, Morton has recruited and trained literally thousands of young men and women, hundreds of whom now hold responsible positions in the conservative movement at national, state and local levels.

Graduates of Morton's training include Terry Dolan of the National Conservative Political Action Committee; Henry Walther, vice president and director of membership services for the National Right to Work Committee and a top New Right leader; Steve Markman, legislative assistant to Sen. Orrin Hatch; Baker Smith, executive director of the tax-deductible Center on National Labor Policy;

Bill Olson, chairman of the Fairfax County (Va.) Republican Committee; Chris Lay, administrative assistant to Congressman Steve Symms; Bob Lauterberg, staff member of the House Republican Study Committee, and John Maxwell, campaign manager for the Grassley for Senate campaign in Iowa.

Morton is optimistic but realistic about the future.

"Conservatives have reached the point," he says, "where we are competitive in political races almost anywhere in the United States. We have reached the point where we can stop a significant percentage of the bad legislation."

But he feels that we are not yet to the point where we can pass legislation we would like to have passed, or repeal legislation we would like to see off the books. The reason is simple.

"We are living in an environment," Morton points out, "where the issues that are taken up are not in our hands. The opposition picks the agenda, and we have to react to it. Until we take one or both of the Houses of Congress, the actual formation of the agenda is going to be out of our hands."

I firmly believe that we are on the brink of capturing one of those Houses, the U.S. Senate, perhaps this year and almost surely by 1982.

Morton is proud of CRYP for having led the way in something that most New Right organizations now insist on—developing their own program of leadership training. He is also typical of New Right leaders who not only plan ahead but analyze what has happened—after the victory or the defeat. And he is a great sharer of ideas and knowledge. Among the New Right, there is a constant cross-fertilization of expertise and information.

Looking ahead to the 1980's, Morton sees larger numbers of conservative movement candidates, and far more technologically proficient candidates.

"They're starting earlier," he reports, "hiring their staff, their pollsters, their media consultants. They're starting earlier to gather the lists of their friends and associates to get them to pledge and work in their campaigns. The candidates who are smart are on the phone early to the national leaders of conservative organizations whether they're broad spectrum groups or focused issue groups."

And invariably, they'll be in touch with Morton Blackwell to find out where to go and whom to see.

Paul Weyrich, Howard Phillips, Terry Dolan, Morton Blackwell are the four who have played the most important roles in the spectacular development of the New Right. But there are others who more than deserve mention for their significant contributions over the years:

• Alan Gottlieb is executive director of the Citizens Committee for the Right to Keep and Bear Arms. Gottlieb's Second Amendment Foundation is a highly effective legal aid group working to stop the liberals' drive to disarm U.S. citizens. A whole cluster of effective New Right groups are rising from Alan's modern facility in Bellevue, Washington.

• Lt. Gen. Daniel Graham (USA-ret.) is the New Right's top national security expert and spokesman. As co-chairman of the Coalition for Peace Through Strength, Dan Graham (a former director of the Defense Intelligence Agency), was one of the three or four most important leaders in our thus-far successful fight against Senate ratification of SALT II. He was also in the forefront of the conservative battles against the Panama Canal treaties and the nomination of Paul Warnke to be director of the Arms Control and Disarmament Agency.

• Reed Larson is president of the National Right to Work Committee, which spearheaded the conservative victories against common situs picketing and the labor law "reform" bill. Reed is an organizational genius who understands how to use, effectively, direct mail, newspaper ads, and other mass media techniques. Henry L. (Huck) Walther is director of membership services and largely responsible for the organization's meteoric growth from 25,000 to its present 1.5 million plus contributors and supporters. I predict Reed's efforts will convince several new states to pass Right to Work laws in the next few years.

• Edwin Feulner is president of the Heritage Foundation, which has become the indispensable think tank for conservatives in Congress and opinion leaders across the nation. Heritage was started in 1973 by Paul Weyrich with major financial help from industrialist Joseph Coors, a courageous conservative. In the last three years under Feulner, Heritage has developed an amazing ability to get the right information to the right people at the right time.

It has gone from an annual budget in 1977 of less than $1 million to more than $4 million in 1980. Heritage now has 55 employees, including research experts on domestic and foreign affairs, and such resident scholars as Russell Kirk and Robert Conquest, the well-known British author.

Essential to Heritage's fast-reacting operation is its key location in three Federal townhouses on Capitol Hill, only five blocks from the Capitol itself. Analyses and backgrounders on current bills are hand-delivered to members of Congress—sometimes within a day of their introduction. Its highly respected *Policy Review* quarterly has been quoted by nearly every major columnist in the nation and used as the basis for thousands of newspaper editorials.

• Daniel J. Popeo is executive director of the Washington Legal Foundation. Sometimes described as the New Right's Ralph Nader, Dan won an epic battle in late 1979 on behalf of Sen. Barry Goldwater when a federal judge ruled that President Carter had illegally stopped the U.S.-Taiwan defense treaty. (Unfortunately, the case was lost on appeal.) Beside Jimmy Carter, Dan Popeo has also taken to court the Democratic National Committee, the General Services Administration, the Federal Mining Enforcement and Safety Administration, and the Federal Election Commission.

• Kathy Teague is executive director of the American Legislative Exchange Council, whose membership includes 600 conservative state legislators. A major ALEC publication is its biennial *Sourcebook of State Legislation*. Tennessee State Rep. Dave Copeland got the idea of a state constitutional tax limitation from ALEC's *Sourcebook* and went on to make Tennessee the first state in the nation to pass such a constitutional amendment in March 1978.

• Lee Edwards, called by the *New York Times* in 1969 the "Voice of the Silent Majority," organized many of the conservative movement's major events in the nation's capital in the sixties and early seventies. Many of the leaders of the New Right were first introduced to each other by Lee or met at events organized by Lee. He was a pioneer in setting the format for the informal style of ad hoc conservative meetings. His luncheons held monthly in downtown D.C. have helped knit together a healthy conservative community. He was an original director of the Committee for Responsible Youth Politics and the first editor of *Conservative Digest.* He wrote the first biography of Ronald Reagan in 1967.

• Gregg Hilton is executive director of the Conservative Victory Fund. Guided by Gregg's near encyclopedic knowledge of campaign facts, the Fund has steadily increased its financial support of conservative candidates, expecting to give $500,000 in 1980.

• Paul Brown is head of the Life Amendment Political Action Committee (LAPAC). Propelled by the Supreme Court's pro-abortion decision in 1973, pro-life forces in America have mushroomed until in 1978, they played a decisive role in the defeats of liberal Senators Dick Clark of Iowa and Tom McIntyre of New Hampshire.

• Judie Brown is president of American Life Lobby, which works in Congress on pro-life issues. She was formerly executive secretary of the National Right to Life Committee, working closely with the brilliant Dr. Mildred Jefferson. Mrs. Brown entered the fight early against the one-sided White House Conference on Families.

She has also helped lead the grassroots attack on the federal Model Adoption Act.

• Peter B. Gemma is national director of National Pro-Life Political Action Committee. Gemma runs the Washington, D.C. office of NPLPAC, headed by Father Charles Fiore, O.P., and his broad campaign experience brings a high level of political sophistication to the pro-life movement.

• David Dennolm is president of the Public Service Research Council. PSRC, with its 150,000 plus supporters, fights the growing power of public employee unions. Denholm's special goal is protecting citizens from police, firemen's, and teachers strikes and the effects of forced collective bargaining between government and public employee unions. PSRC led the successful fight against liberalizing the Hatch Act, which restricts political activity by federal government workers.

• David Keene, a former national chairman of Young Americans for Freedom, is active on many conservative fronts, serving as consultant to the National Tax Limitation Committee — director of the American Conservative Union — and on the advisory board of the Washington Legal Foundation. Keene was southern coordinator for the Reagan for President Committee in 1976 and was also a consultant to the National Conservative Political Action Committee in 1978.

• Rhonda Stahlman is chairman of Conservatives Against Liberal Legislation (CALL), a New Right, multi-issue lobbying group which is developing heavyweight ability to influence the legislative process. Rhonda was an officer of the

Committee for Responsible Youth Politics and then of the National Conservative Political Action Committee. A dedicated Christian activist, she played a major role in bringing fundamentalist leaders like Dr. Bob Billings, with whom she worked in Indiana, into the New Right.

• Lewis Uhler is chairman of the National Tax Limitation Committee, which now claims more than 100 Congressional co-sponsors of its constitutional amendment limiting federal spending to a declining share of the gross national product. The Committee has 500,000 financial supporters and an annual budget of more than $4 million.

• And last, but certainly not least, there is Phyllis Schlafly, founder and national chairman of Stop ERA. Phyllis is also president of the Eagle Forum, a national organization of conservative women, author of nine books, syndicated columnist, former CBS Radio commentator, wife and mother of six children, an attorney, a debater without equal—the heart and soul of a women's movement which believes in family, God and country.

She and her determined group of housewives and mothers have taken on and defeated the entire U.S. establishment, including three U.S. presidents, the Congress, the news media, organized labor, the foundations, and every liberal group you can name, from Common Cause to the National Organization of Women.

Phyllis is an excellent example of a true leader.

Phyllis did not stop ERA by simply making speeches, debating, writing books, articles and newsletters.

Of course, she did all of these things and did them well, but conservatives have been doing these things for years and losing almost every battle.

Phyllis set out to organize the anti-ERA movement.

She called meetings of her state officers, and they developed strategy as to how they would present their testimony before an upcoming legislative hearing. They would develop ideas on how to get media attention. They would determine which legislators needed to receive hundreds of letters and phone calls.

They would call for mass meetings of their supporters on the steps of each state capitol.

In other words, they developed a plan of action to win and implemented their plan with intelligent and hard work.

If Phyllis had only engaged in debates, speech making and writing, ERA would be the 27th Amendment to the U.S. Constitution.

Phyllis Schlafly would be the first to say that ERA has been stopped because of tens of thousands of hard working women and men volunteers.

But without this brilliant leader calling meetings and organizing the opposition, a million volunteers could not have stopped the liberal juggernaut from passing ERA.

There are dozens of conservative movement activists in public office—in the U.S. Senate, in the U.S. House of Representatives and in state legislatures across the nation. I cannot list them all, but here are a few who are always seeking to build the conservative movement— who have taken a leadership role in crucial New

Right battles—who are determined not just to put up a good fight but to win:

• Senator Orrin G. Hatch of Utah. A former tax lawyer and union member, Orrin led the successful battles against labor law "reform," IRS harassment of Christian schools and federal funding of abortions.

• Senator Jesse A. Helms of North Carolina. I feel that just as Robert Taft was known as Mr. Republican, we will soon see Jesse Helms become known as Mr. Conservative. Jesse *is* the conscience of the conservative movement. He has introduced an amendment permitting prayer in public schools which may become law soon. He led the battle against Senate rules changes that would have strengthened the majority leader's power. He has commanded countless foreign policy battles, including Rhodesia, Nicaragua and Taiwan. He initiated the campaign to grant honorary U.S. citizenship to Alexander Solzhenitsyn. He has a number of important movement conservatives on his staff, such as Dr. James Lucier and John Carbaugh, who have gained national reputations.

• Sen. Paul Laxalt of Nevada. He was the very effective leader in our battle against Senate ratification of the Panama Canal treaties, winning praise for his grace and good humor from friend and foe alike. He was national chairman for Ronald Reagan's presidential campaign in 1976 and again in 1980. He also led the fight against instant voter registration and taxpayer financing of Congressional elections.

• Sen. James McClure of Idaho. As chairman of the influential Senate Steering Committee, McClure speaks softly but carries a big stick. He has made a specialty of energy, exposing the elitism of the environmental movement and the fanaticism of the antinuclear forces.

• Congressman Philip Crane of Illinois. Phil waged a tireless campaign for the Republican nomination for President from 1978-80, carrying the conservative message to millions of Americans. He chaired the American Conservative Union from 1977-79, during the period of its greatest growth. As ACU chairman, he organized and hosted monthly ecumenical luncheons which greatly helped old and new conservatives to work out their personal tactics and strategy differences. A major factor in Phil's effectiveness was Rich Williamson, who was Phil's principal political adviser for many years and who continues to contribute significantly to the conservative movement.

• Congressman Robert Dornan of California, an electrifying public speaker who originated the idea for the POW-MIA bracelet in 1970 when he was a Los Angeles broadcaster. Over 5 million bracelets were distributed. Congressman Dornan was active in stopping the transfer of Cyber 76 advanced computers to Soviet Russia and has fought hard for the B-1 bomber.

• Congressman Mickey Edwards of Oklahoma, who followed Winston Churchill's advice to never never give up. Mickey ran and narrowly lost in 1974, receiving 48.3% of the vote. He ran and won narrowly in 1976, receiving almost exactly half the vote. But he put it all together in 1978, winning reelection with 80% of the vote, including over 75% of the black and labor vote.

• Congressman Newt Gingrich of Georgia, who has emerged as a principal spokesman for the conservative coalition in Congress. Gingrich showed his leadership ability in November 1979 when he organized bi-partisan support for an alternative to the White House-Speaker Tip O'Neill budget. He narrowly lost by a vote of 205-190, an impressive showing for a freshman Republican against the combined power of the White House, Speaker O'Neill and the rest of the Democratic leadership.

• Congressman Steve Symms of Idaho. Steve is a libertarian conservative who is challenging Sen. Frank Church in 1980. A farmer who practices free enterprise, Steve is an American who understands the importance of maintaining peace and security through strength.

• Democratic Congressman Larry McDonald is from Jimmy Carter's Georgia, but he voted against Carter more than any other Member in the 95th Congress. Larry is always out in front on domestic and national security issues and is pressing to restore the House Internal Security Committee. He is dedicated to building the conservative movement nationally and is generous in the giving of his time and talent.

• California State Sen. H. L. (Bill) Richardson founded both Gun Owners of America and Gun Owners of California in 1975 and has built them into highly effective political operations. Together the organizations have over a hundred thousand supporters and annual budgets of more than a million dollars.

And so, starting in 1974, we worked long and hard to build a new conservative movement. We were far from perfect. We made mistakes. In

1976, we backed some losing candidates, but also key winners like Orrin Hatch.

But on balance we had impact. We learned by our mistakes and we weren't afraid to make mistakes. We began to be noticed. We were written up in the national media and torn down by nervous liberals.

Here's an example of how we made them not only nervous but worried.

In March of 1977, Jimmy Carter proposed four changes in our election laws.

They were: (1) have the taxpayers finance all Congressional elections; (2) allow any voter to vote on election day if they showed up with most any kind of identification; (3) change the Hatch Act to allow Federal employees to actively participate in politics; (4) change the U.S. Constitution to allow for the direct election of the President and do away with the electoral college.

A few weeks later at about 10:15 one night, my phone rang. It was Paul Weyrich.

He said he had just attended a meeting of conservative Republican Senators. He said they had come to the conclusion that even though these election law changes would hurt the Republican Party, there was nothing they could do to stop it — most felt that they were ideas whose time had come.

I told Paul that I felt the New Right could develop the strategy to stop Carter's plan.

I also reminded Paul that it was late, that he had waked me up and that I would call him in the morning.

I called him the next morning, and we decided to have a meeting once a week in my conference room with about 15 key New Right leaders.

We quickly developed our strategy. Then week after week (sometimes we met more than once a week) we developed and implemented our tactics.

We made mailings to large Republican contributors, asking them to call wavering Senators. We arranged for Op-Ed pieces in major newspapers. We held briefings with the press to explain our position. We mailed millions of letters, asking that phone calls, cards and letters be sent to Congress.

We also used smart public relations wherever we could.

For example, Congressmen Steve Symms and Robert Dornan got national coverage in July 1977 with dummy ID cards (the brainstorm of Dick Dingman at a meeting in my conference room) to demonstrate the possibilities for fraud in Carter's instant voter registration plan.

The ID cards each had the photos of either Symms or Dornan but the names of liberal Democrats on the House Administration Committee who supported Carter's plan. The reporters and the photographers loved it, particularly when liberal Committee Chairman Frank Thompson blew his top in public over the ID's.

The *Washington Star* published an enormous five-column photo on page one of the phony ID's, which had been blown up to poster size for a news conference.

On that day, Carter's plan to let anyone vote who turned up at the polls with just about any kind of paper showing he lived in that voting district died and has not been heard from since.

The liberal National Committee For An Effective Congress was opposed to one portion of the campaign finance bill, and Common Cause opposed Carter's proposed changes in the Hatch Act. So we worked with both of these liberal organizations in the area that concerned them.

Senator Paul Laxalt worked with many businessmen to urge them to pressure Congress.

Laxalt agreed to coordinate the effort inside the Senate. He organized and led a successful filibuster that for weeks defeated the best efforts of President Carter, Senate Majority Leader Bobby Byrd, Teddy Kennedy and other liberals to pass taxpayer financing of Congressional elections. And on August 2, 1977 the liberals threw in the towel.

This was the New Right at its best.

About 50 of us got together in September, 1977 at a dinner in Washington to celebrate David's victory over Goliath.

Now three and a half years after Carter introduced his plans to change the election laws that were designed to put the conservatives out of business. not a change has been made.

This was probably the first major victory of the New Right. A rag-tag group of New Right conservatives had done what Republican Senators said could not be done.

We had our first taste of victory. And there was no stopping us now.

U.S. News & World Report said about us in July 1977: "A third force is quietly building a political apparatus that pointedly disregards party labels."

The *New York Times* said in December 1977: "The New Right. . . is more tightly organized, better financed, more sophisticated and more pragmatic than their predecessors."

Eddie Mahe, then executive director of the Republican National Committee, commented in June 1977: "If you ranked political institutions in this country, organized labor would be first. The Democratic Party is second. The Republican Party is third. [The New Right] is unquestionably fourth."

Lyn Nofziger, director of communications, Reagan for President Committee: "The old right were talkers and pamphleteers. They would just as soon go down in flames as win. But the New Right has moved toward a more pragmatic goal of accomplishing things."

One of the major differences in this group of new conservatives was that we weren't afraid to try even if there was only a 20% chance of success.

We weren't worried about how the establishment, the press and others would view us if we lost. We knew if you expected to hit a lot of home runs, you had to expect to strike out a lot.

Remember that in 1927, when Babe Ruth led the major leagues with 60 home runs, he also led in strikeouts with 89.

Between 1974 and 1978, the New Right received a lot of criticism from other conservatives who felt that we were wasting our time and dividing the resources of the conservative movement by moving in new directions and starting new publications, new political action committees, new research foundations, and new public interest law firms. They were greatly concerned about our massive use of technology such as computerized direct mail.

We have won by being firm and aggressive. Our language at times makes more gentle sorts nervous. But this is the way of most all successful political movements.

It's easy to complain about this or that thing that the New Right has done. In fact, there are lots of things we've done that we would do differently now, things we'd like to retract, words we'd like to pull back.

But to those conservatives who complain about mistakes the New Right has made, I ask, "Would you prefer that conservatives go back to the way we did things 10 years ago?"

Those few who complain and like to highlight our shortcomings remind me of the story about the man whose car motor stopped at the traffic light. When the light turned green, he still couldn't get the car started and the man next in line started honking his car horn. After a minute or so of this, the man whose motor wouldn't start got out of his car and went to the man sitting in the car behind him who was honking.

And he suggested that they change jobs. He said, "I'll honk your car horn and you go start my car."

Those who feel they could do it better, let them step forward. I for one will gladly turn over my pressure cooker-type life, 12-hour days, 70-hour weeks to anyone who can be more effective.

But unless you've shown that you know how to take control of this country from Big Media, Big Business, Big Labor, Big Government, then show a little patience with and understanding for those who have proven that they just might be able to do it.

While almost no one (myself included) likes to be criticized, especially unfairly and by those with whom you share a common goal, we were convinced we were doing the right thing.

We also knew that if we were successful, few would remember the criticism and the negative media coverage. If we were unsuccessful, we felt freedom in America and around the world would be reduced and even lost.

All the while, the pressure on us to perform more and more effectively became greater and greater.

By late 1977, the liberals had clearly picked their strategy to try to finish us off. They said that if the New Right didn't come up with a couple of really big wins in 1978, we would be exposed as all smoke and no fire.

But we were ready, and confident. And 1978 *was* a crucial turning point in the history of the New Right, and perhaps in our nation's history as well. Ironically, our greatest victories came as a result of a battle we lost — the Panama Canal treaties.

V

1978: Our Critical Year

No political issue in the last 25 years so clearly divided the American establishment and the American people as the Panama Canal treaties.

In favor of the treaties were the Carter administration, the Democratic leadership in both Houses of Congress, both living ex-Presidents (six U.S. Presidents helped negotiate the treaties), Big Labor, Big Business, Big Media, the big international banks, and just about every liberal political and cultural star you could name.

Against the treaties were the American people — as many as 75% of them, according to the polls. Probably over 85% of registered Republicans opposed the giveaway of the Panama Canal.

And yet, the Republican Party refused to take the leadership in opposing the treaties. So the New Right picked up the flag and set out to do battle with the American establishment.

In November 1977, I said publicly that the Panama Canal was a "no-loss" issue for conservatives. I predicted that it would not only rally conservatives but bring countless members of the Silent Majority into the conservative movement. I called the Canal "the most electrifying issue conservatives have ever had."

Ronald Reagan made the Canal a major issue during the 1976 Republican Presidential primaries, declaring: "The Canal is ours. We built it. We paid for it. And we intend to keep it."

And the Panama Canal in turn saved Reagan from certain defeat. Governor Reagan was not a viable Presidential candidate after his defeat in the Florida primary.

Then two things happened: (1) Sen. Jesse Helms and his longtime political adviser Tom Ellis took over the running of Reagan's primary campaign in North Carolina and (2) Reagan decided to make the Panama Canal a major issue between himself and President Ford. As a result, he won the North Carolina primary, got back on the offensive and almost won the Presidential nomination.

Other conservative spokesmen detailed the strategic importance of the Canal — the Marxist commitment of Panamanian dictator Omar Torrijos — the $10 billion investment of the American people in the Canal — and the importance of the Canal as a preeminent symbol of America's "can-do" spirit.

As columnist Patrick J. Buchanan wrote in January 1978:

"The Panama Canal is the right issue at the right time in the right place to say, 'Thus far and no farther.' A political war to the death over the Canal treaty could realign American politics, reinvigorate a weakened spirit of nationalism, and if lost, do for those who surrendered the Canal what Yalta did for the Democratic Party."

Exactly what we had in mind.

The left won the Senate vote on the Panama Canal. But it was a very costly battle and it may be a major factor in their losing the war.

At the heart of the campaign was the close cooperation between anti-treaty forces in the U.S. Senate (the "inside" team) and forces generating grassroots opposition to the treaties (the "outside" team). The key man was Sen. Paul Laxalt of Nevada, whose competence and composure under pressure won respect on all sides.

Laxalt held frequent meetings — which became daily as the battle warmed up — at which anti-treaty Senators, New Right leaders Paul Weyrich, Howard Phillips and Terry Dolan, public relations expert William Rhatican, representatives of the Senate Steering Committee and other New Right leaders would decide the best tactics to win over undecided Senators.

At the same time, the "outside" team was carrying out the most intense issue-oriented political campaign in our nation in decades. We wound up coordinating our activities with nearly 20 national organizations, an exercise in coalition building none of us will ever forget.

There were endless brainstorming sessions about the best approach to each undecided Senator, which mailing lists to use against which Senator, which primary or general election challenger of a pro-treaty Senator to encourage.

For example, someone suggested that Jack Eckerd, the Florida Republican gubernatorial candidate, contact Florida Democratic Sen. Richard Stone.

Terry Dolan decided that NCPAC would write 10,000 leading Republicans urging them to tell Howard Baker that a pro-treaty vote would ruin his presidential hopes.

Information was made available to State Rep. Woody Jenkins of Louisiana, whose major U.S. Senate primary effort helped force incumbent Democrat J. Bennett Johnston to vote against the treaties.

Those were long days and long nights. Some would begin with an 8 a.m. breakfast at my home in McLean, Va., and end at 10 p.m. with a leadership meeting somewhere else in the Washington area. Thousands of telephone calls, including scores of conference calls, were made at all hours.

Raw numbers will give you some idea of our efforts. The Conservative Caucus under Howard Phillips mailed 3 million letters and conducted anti-treaty rallies and campaigns in all 50 states. Terry Dolan's National Conservative Political Action Committee sent out almost half a million letters.

John Fisher's American Security Council mailed 2 million letters. The Council on Inter-American Security, under Ronald Docksai and L. Francis Bouchey, mailed 2 million letters, and broadcast radio spots in 13 states.

The American Conservative Union's half-hour TV documentary on the Panama Canal reached an estimated 10 million viewers, and raised $1 million. ACU also mailed 2 million letters.

And a "Truth Squad" featuring Senators Paul Laxalt, Jake Garn and Bill Scott, Congressmen Phil Crane, Larry McDonald and Mickey

Edwards, and two dozen other political and military leaders reached over 10 million Americans through TV and newspaper coverage of their appearances in key states.

I volunteered to raise the money for the Truth Squad. We mailed 5,000 letters and raised over $110,000. Several conservative groups also contributed $5,000 each, including The Conservative Caucus, the American Security Council, the Committee for the Survival of a Free Congress, National Conservative Political Action Committee, Citizens for the Republic, the American Conservative Union, and the Richard A. Viguerie Company.

This money was used to finance a chartered Boeing 737 jet, broadcast radio ads on the status of undecided Senators, run newspaper ads and distribute information about the Canal.

The Truth Squad trip in late January and early February 1978 was organized by Bill Rhatican and resembled a White House campaign trip. The travelling party, which covered more than 6,000 miles in less than four days, included 30 representatives of the national news media.

There were major news conferences at each of the four stops—Miami, St. Louis, Denver and Portland, Ore.—and each time conservatives received excellent local and national coverage.

The Truth Squad trip was a prime example of how conservatives were learning invaluable lessons in the political major leagues — lessons which we would put to good use later in 1978.

A few months earlier, Phil Crane, Rich Williamson and I decided that we needed a good readable book on the Panama Canal. I agreed to publish it. And so in January 1978, 100,000 paperback copies of *Surrender in Panama* by Congressman Philip M. Crane came out. Copies were sent to just about every important media person and political leader in the country. It was another example of how the New Right operates when it goes into high gear.

While all this was going on, the Republican National Committee was mailing out millions of letters signed by Ronald Reagan asking people to contribute to the RNC in an effort to defeat the Panama Canal treaties. Approximately $700,000 was raised.

But when Paul Laxalt asked RNC Chairman Bill Brock for $50,000 to help underwrite the cost of the Truth Squad, the RNC chairman refused. The outrageous fact is that Brock refused to spend any of the money raised by Reagan's anti-treaty letter on any anti-treaty activities.

At their insistence, Laxalt and Reagan talked with Brock on December 15, 1977 via a joint telephone call and came away very angry. Brock would not budge. Someone present during this conversation said he heard Reagan use words that he didn't know Reagan knew.

Almost immediately, Senator Laxalt and Congressman Phil Crane, then chairman of the American Conservative Union, called me, and I volunteered to raise the $50,000 that Bill Brock and the Republican National Committee wouldn't give them.

Their call was one more proof of the reduced importance of political parties. And of the New Right's ability to engage in and finance important political activity outside a major political party.

I assured Laxalt and Crane that I could do the fund-raising in two weeks time. But instead of raising $50,000, over $110,000 came in. I was assisted greatly on the mailing by Morton Blackwell, who volunteered his time and expertise as did I. We mailed two letters in one envelope — the first signed by Ronald Reagan and the second by Paul Laxalt. The extraordinary results confirmed that conservatives across the country felt as strongly about the Panama Canal as any issue in my lifetime.

Between the summer of 1977 and April 1978 when the final Senate votes occurred, the New Right sent between 7 and 9 million cards and letters to Americans asking them to: visit or write their Senators to express their views against the giveaway, write letters to newspaper editors, call in to TV and radio talk shows, ask organizations they belonged to to pass anti-Treaty resolutions, and send money so we could reach more Americans.

In all, the New Right spent about $3 million in an all-out effort to help save the Canal. We almost pulled it off.

The New Right fought Big Government, Big Business, Big Labor and Big Media to a standstill, for almost two years.

At the beginning of the battle, about 70% of the American people supported the New Right's position.

And after two years, we still had about 70% of the American people with us.

If I were the establishment, I would be worried. A handful of New Right conservatives almost beat them.

But mere numbers do not tell the whole story of the many individual sacrifices demanded and made.

Howard Phillips, the nearest thing to a perpetual motion machine that the New Right has, organized through The Conservative Caucus more than 12 major Keep-Our-Canal rallies, a nationwide billboard campaign, radio and TV spots, a phone bank, countless press conferences and speeches, and anti-Treaty campaigns in all 50 states.

Conservative Caucus field men slept in airports and bus stations while doing advance work for these events.

Terry Dolan and Paul Weyrich were unceasing in their lobbying efforts, urging their hundreds of thousands of supporters to contact their Senators and coaching their political candidates on how to make the most of the Canal issue.

Bill Rhatican, an expert publicist highly regarded for his sense of news and his ability to keep cool and good-humored in a crisis, skillfully guided the outside team's meetings.

John Laxalt, the Washington representative of Reagan's Citizens for the Republic, was of invaluable help to both the outside and inside teams.

On March 16, 1978, and again on April 18, 1978, we fell just two votes short. Needing 34 Senators to say "no," the Senate by a narrow margin of 68—32 voted to give away the Panama Canal. But the New Right did not really lose. Our "defeat" became a victory seven months later when the American people went to the polls.

Our campaign to save the Canal gained conservative converts around the country — added more than 400,000 new names to our lists — encouraged many of the movement's leading figures (like Gordon Humphrey of New Hampshire) to run for public office — and produced significant liberal defeats in the fall.

In fact, 13 incumbent Senators who voted for the treaties in 1978 did not return to the Senate in 1979. Eight were defeated at the polls.

The New Right came out of the Panama Canal fight with no casualties, not even a scar.

Because of Panama we are better organized. We developed a great deal of confidence in ourselves, and our opponents became weaker.

That November, the New Right really came of age.

For weeks, press speculation had mounted over the showing we would make. If we elected a good number of conservatives, we would be hailed as a major force in American politics. If not, liberals would begin writing our political obituary.

Frankly, the election returns exceeded even our most optimistic expectations. There were many victories we savored that night, but probably the two sweetest and unexpected by most political experts were those of Gordon Humphrey in New Hampshire and Roger Jepsen in Iowa.

Gordon Humphrey was the first U.S. Senator to come up through the ranks of the New Right. He was the newest of political newcomers, an Allegheny Airlines co-pilot until he announced for the Senate. At 37, Humphrey had never before run for public office, and had lived in New Hampshire only four years.

When Humphrey decided to run against veteran Democratic incumbent Tom McIntyre, he had little more than his personal life's savings to spend and the steadfast support of the many people he had met as New Hampshire state coordinator for The Conservative Caucus.

He was virtually unknown among the New Hampshire political establishment and given almost no chance to win.

But Humphrey proved his vote-getting ability, and surprised a lot of politicians, by receiving more votes in the GOP primary than his three opponents combined.

Humphrey campaigned across New Hampshire as a New Right conservative. "I want to be the toughest skinflint in the United States Senate," he said in his TV ads.

He was tough all the way — against gun control, against wasteful government spending. "I don't consider my role," he declared, "to see how much I can loot from the Federal treasury."

Each Senatorial candidate turned the election into a referendum.

Humphrey's referendum was McIntyre's vote to give away the Panama Canal and his overall liberal voting record.

McIntyre's referendum was the New Right. He attacked us on the floor of the U.S. Senate, on national television (via the "Today" show) and all across New Hampshire.

The people of New Hampshire backed Gordon Humphrey's referendum and rejected that of McIntyre, who after his defeat published a book attacking the New Right.

I must add here that Gordon might not have gotten across his New Right message and beaten his opponent without the superb assistance and, for a time, campaign management of Terry Dolan. When almost everyone else concluded McIntyre was unbeatable, Terry dug in harder, insisting Gordon Humphrey could win.

It was Terry Dolan who came up with the technique of aiming Boston TV at New Hampshire voters—an approach rejected by past campaign managers as too expensive and too "wasteful" in its impact. But Terry had learned through surveys and polls that thousands of new New Hampshire voters had recently moved from Massachusetts and were accustomed to watching Boston stations.

On election day, Gordon Humphrey pulled off the year's biggest political upset, defeating a 16-year incumbent senior senator 51—49%.

The political situation in Iowa was different. Republican Roger Jepsen was a former two-term lieutenant governor. For over a decade, he had been the state's leading conservative. He thought he had retired from politics (at a youthful 49), but decided to challenge Democratic Senator Dick Clark, feeling that the incumbent was just too liberal for Iowa.

In fact, the liberal Americans for Democratic Action identified Dick Clark as the most liberal member of the Senate. As chairman of the Africa subcommittee of the Senate Foreign Relations Committee, Clark was U.N. Ambassador Andrew Young's chief legislative supporter. The American Conservative Union gave Clark a conservative rating of 4%—worse than George McGovern's.

But in Iowa, Clark posed as a conservative, talking fiscal responsibility and limited government wherever he went.

So Jepsen hammered away at Clark for what he was—a big-spending liberal who voted one way in Washington and talked another way back home.

And the New Right turned out in force to help Jepsen. My company did the direct mail for him. Paul Weyrich's Committee for the Survival of a Free Congress and Terry Dolan's National Conservative Political Action Committee and Morton Blackwell's Committee for Responsible Youth Politics assisted him.

Right to Life groups heavily backed Jepsen, hitting hard at Clark's pro-abortion record.

The National Right to Work Committee did mailings and ran newspaper ads, comparing Clark's anti-Right to Work and Jepsen's pro-Right to Work stands—an important issue in a Right to Work state like Iowa.

Jepsen's aggressive hard-hitting campaign drove the truth home, and on November 7, 1978, he beat Dick Clark by 52% to 48%, adding another leaf to New Right laurels.

Other first-time winners for the New Right in the U.S. Senate were Bill Armstrong in Colorado, John Warner in Virginia and Alan Simpson in Wyoming. I must also mention one defeat—Jeff Bell in New Jersey.

Although Jeff lost to Democrat Bill Bradley in the general election, he beat aging veteran liberal Sen. Clifford Case in the Republican primary. Few thought Jeff had a chance, although *The New Right Report* flatly predicted in January that Case would be defeated in 1978.

Jeff Bell told me that he could not have beaten Case and run as well as he did against Bradley without the enthusiastic nation-wide support of the New Right.

In the U.S. House of Representatives, conservatives also made sizeable gains. About 25 new GOP congressmen came from within the New Right ranks or became new supporters of the conservative movement.

And about 18 new Democratic conservatives won election. One of them, New Right Congressman Kent Hance of Texas, was elected president of the Democratic freshman class. They are Democrats who have good ties to the conservative movement, owe nothing to Big Labor bosses and have largely avoided links with the Carter administration. Many of these Democrats received significant aid from New Right groups, usually in primaries.

Among these new Congressmen in both parties were Carroll Campbell from South Carolina, Bill Carney and Jerry Solomon from New York, Newt Gingrich of Georgia, Phil Gramm and Ron Paul from Texas, Jim Jeffries from Kansas, Ken Kramer from Colorado and Bill Dannemeyer from California.

How did the New Right help swing these victories?

1. The most important single factor was the involvement of record numbers of new people on behalf of conservative candidates. Hundreds of thousands of people, for the first time in their lives, contributed to conservative candidates. Dedicated, concerned Americans who gave $1000, $100 or $10 made a big difference. These personal contributions were, by far,

the largest source of funds for conservative candidates.

A handful of dedicated people like Weyrich, Dolan and others worked night and day to make this happen in 1978 — in contrast with the unorganized efforts of conservatives a decade earlier.

2. The level of competence in conservative campaigns shot up dramatically. It was no accident. Dozens of conservative political action committees (PACs), conservative lobbying groups and educational organizations held approximately a hundred training schools and seminars on the political process and how to win elections in 1977-78. The schools were held all over the country, so a large pool of talented, trained conservatives was available almost everywhere.

Among the most active training programs were those sponsored by the Committee for the Survival of a Free Congress, the National Conservative Political Action Committee, Citizens for the Republic and the Committee for Responsible Youth Politics.

3. Conservative PACs made their campaign commitments carefully. When a race looked winnable, extra help and extra bucks were given.

New Right leaders made phone calls to corporate PACs telling them a certain campaign was winnable. Direct mail, public relations and polling help were brought in for late and close elections.

National Stop-ERA, pro-gun, pro-life, Right to Work and other New Right leaders would contact their local members. Word was passed to ministers to get the message to their parishioners.

In contrast to previous years, very little conservative PAC help in 1978 went to unwinnable campaigns, no matter how "good" a conservative a candidate might have been.

For example, CSFC under Paul Weyrich spent $400,000 to help elect 31 conservative candidates — one of the best yields per dollar of any political group in the country.

Seventy percent of the candidates supported by Terry Dolan's NCPAC won, prompting the AFL-CIO's COPE to mourn:

"NCPAC . . . has created for the first time in our political history, an organizational base for the Right that is in place and ready for action at a moment's notice in any campaign, at any level, anywhere in the country."

4. Conservative single-interest groups (pro-gun, pro-life, Right to Work, etc.) were effective. They attracted hundreds of thousands of previously uninvolved people into campaign activity. They made specially targeted mailings . . . held training schools . . . bought advertising exposing liberal voting records in their special interest publications . . . spent generously on purely lobbying and educational activities which raised public consciousness of their issues.

For example, after Mass on the Sunday before the November 7, 1978, election, most Iowa Catholics were handed a pamphlet contrasting Dick Clark's pro-abortion votes with Roger Jepsen's anti-abortion position.

In my opinion, the nation owes a major debt to single-purpose groups in the areas of Right to Work, Right to Life, tax limitation, defense and pro-gun activity.

5. More than in past years, growing numbers of business and association PACs spent their

money wisely on free enterprise and national defense candidates. But many business PACs still showered their money on liberal incumbents and even liberal challengers.

However, one of the major accomplishments of the New Right has been to swing corporate and association PACs from heavily supporting liberals toward a much greater role in helping conservatives.

The following analysis by *The New Right Report* shows a significant shift by four such PACs between 1976 and 1978. The % shows how much money the PACs of these groups gave to liberals in contested races for the U.S. House and Senate.

	1976	1978
Chicago & Northwestern Transportation Company	92.9% liberal	27% liberal
National Forest Products Association	100.0% liberal	39% liberal
Weyerhaeuser Corporation	61.9% liberal	17% liberal
Georgia Pacific	44.8% liberal	16% liberal

In 1980, we expect the support of conservative rather than liberal candidates by corporate and association PACs to be even greater.

6. Conservative activity was not limited to GOP candidates. Involvement in Democratic politics by conservative activists was a major development for the conservative cause in 1978.

In some cases, conservative Democrats had little or no GOP opposition. In other cases, supposedly unbeatable liberal Democrats were upset by conservative Democrats running conservative campaigns (backed by the New Right) in the primary.

In 1978, the New Right discovered that there is more than one way to skin a liberal in a campaign.

There was the Jesse Helms example. By his devoted efforts on behalf of almost every conservative cause during his first term, Senator Helms of North Carolina became a hero of the conservative movement. In his 1978 reelection campaign, a strong direct mail effort attracted about $7 million from 190,000 contributors, including 30,000 in North Carolina. These mailings, begun two years before his reelection, enabled the Helms campaign to organize at every level for an almost unprecedented grassroots effort.

There was the Mickey Edwards example. Before his 2,644 vote victory in 1976, Congressman Edwards of Oklahoma and his wife Sue personally knocked on more than 40,000 doors in his district. Such personal contact builds lasting ties. In Congress, Mickey paid a lot of personal attention to all voters in his district, especially black voters.

He convinced them that conservative ideas are the best ideas in the long run for all Americans. He showed, for example, how the liberal-imposed minimum wage increases unemployment among young blacks. As a result, Mickey Edwards won reelection in 1978 with 80% of the vote, including 75% of both black and labor voters.

There was the Bob Kasten example. Former Congressman Robert Kasten of Wisconsin developed a volunteer recruitment plan which enabled him, in his U.S. House races, to enlist a large number of enthusiastic workers. These volunteers then organized an intensive voter identification drive, finding and persuading enough voters to elect Kasten repeatedly to Congress.

In 1976 and 1978, largely through the Committee for the Survival of a Free Congress, many conservative candidates used the Kasten plan to win nominations and elections. For example, Bruce Erickson, campaign manager for Republican Jim Jeffries, who upset liberal Congresswoman Martha Keys (D—Kan.), says flatly: "It was the (Kasten plan) organization which pulled us through."

Ironically, Bob neglected to use his own plan in the GOP primary when he ran for governor of Wisconsin in 1978. As a result, he lost the GOP primary because he was waiting for the November general election before starting the Kasten plan.

These techniques were used by the New Right in 1978 to become a major force in American politics.

We won far more than a number of important races in the U.S. Senate and House of Representatives. We helped shift the entire spectrum of politics to the right.

I doubt that a dozen liberal candidates for Congress, if they were strongly challenged, admitted they were liberals.

Incumbents with the most left-wing records proclaimed they were against deficits, red tape and interfering bureaucrats. Veteran liberals suddenly sang the praises of free enterprise and a strong national defense. They knew they had to, or go down to certain defeat.

The conservative momentum achieved in 1978 has not subsided but has increased.

Conservatives will dominate the 1980's, I predict, because most of our leaders are now coming into their own, while most of the liberal leaders are dead, retired or just too tired to compete in the demanding decade before us.

VI

The Four Keys to
Our Success

Our success is built on four elements — single issue groups, multi-issue conservative groups, coalition politics and direct mail.

Conservative single issue groups have been accused of not only fragmenting American politics but threatening the very existence of our two-party system. Congressman David Obey of Wisconsin, a liberal Democrat, has even charged that government has nearly been brought to a standstill by single issue organizations.

Nonsense!

In the first place, all the New Right has done is copy the success of the old left.

Liberal single issue groups were around long before we were, and the liberals still have as many or more than we do.

Civil rights was a single issue that Hubert Humphrey used to rise to national office. The Vietnam War was a single issue that George

McGovern used to rise to national prominence. The environment, consumerism, anti-nuclear power — these are all single issues around which liberals have organized and exercised power and influence.

In the area of public interest law, liberal groups such as the Environmental Defense Fund, the National Prison Project, the Mexican-American Legal Defense and Education Fund, the Southern Poverty Law Center, the National Veterans Law Center, the Women's Legal Defense Fund have drastically changed the direction of the Federal government.

Ralph Nader is nothing if not a collection of single issues. The liberals who are upset now about conservative single issue groups were not upset about the groups pushing for legalization of marijuana ... homosexual rights ... or ERA.

As columnist John Roche, a former chairman of the liberal Americans for Democratic Action, wrote in June 1980 about single issue groups:

"The conservatives learned to play from us. The labor movement, for example, employed one-issue politics with spectacular success for years. Like my grandpa, they would have supported a baboon if it endorsed increasing the minimum wage."

And as columnists Jack Germond and Jules Witcover wrote in the *Washington Star*:

"By taking such an approach, the conservatives are essentially following the same strategy that made the liberal coalition in the Democratic Party the dominant force in our politics over the last several decades."

And as columnist John Chamberlain wrote: "The technique of coalition building is open to anybody. It is as old as American politics. . . Let's have no tears about it—it will continue to be the way in America as long as the republic stands."

Here are just some of the better known liberal single issue groups:

- Sierra Club
- National Organization of Women (NOW)
- Congressional Black Caucus
- Planned Parenthood
- SANE
- Gay Rights National Lobby
- National Abortion Rights Action League
- Public Citizen (Ralph Nader's key organization)
- Wilderness Society
- Women Strike for Peace

Could it be the real reason why they're upset is that conservative single issue groups are becoming more and more effective and having more and more impact on the political process, as in the 1978 defeat of liberals Dick Clark, Tom McIntyre and others?

Senator George McGovern says he fails to understand voters who would look at only one issue in a Senator's record while ignoring all the other issues. That's because McGovern is worried about reelection in 1980 and right to life forces are a large part of his worry. "But McGovern was singing quite another tune," Paul Weyrich reminds us, "when he encouraged leftist groups to make the war *the* issue that counted 10 years ago."

And there is far less liberal legislation being passed in the Congress as a result of conservative single issue groups. Liberal proposals like labor law "reform," consumer protection, common situs picketing, changes in the Hatch Act, instant voter registration and taxpayer financing of Congressional elections were stopped dead by conservative opposition.

Second, single issue groups naturally emerge because the political parties run away from issues. Single issue groups are the result *of* not the reason *for* the decline of political parties.

If one of the two major political parties had concerned itself more with issues like right to life, high taxes, the growth of the federal government, the right to keep and bear arms, a strong national defense, prayer in the schools, strengthening the family, sex on TV and in the movies, there probably would not have been an explosion of conservative single issue groups.

For example, between 70-75% of the American public opposed giving our Panama Canal to a Marxist dictator. And probably about 85% of Republicans opposed the giveaway.

What was the official and unofficial position of the Republican National Committee? They wanted nothing to do with the issue.

However, the RNC didn't mind raising more than $700,000 from conservative Republicans by sending out fund raising letters asking for money to defeat the Panama Canal.

But when Ronald Reagan and Paul Laxalt went to the chairman of the Republican National Committee in December 1977 to ask for $50,000 to fight the Panama Canal giveaway, they were told that the Republican party was going to stay away from this controversial issue. (See Chapter 5.)

And in 1978 we saw Senator Robert Packwood, chairman of the Senate Republican Campaign Committee, supervising the raising of large sums of money from conservative Republicans (again via direct mail) on the single issue of labor law reform and the general subject of abuses of power by Washington union officials.

But how did Senator Packwood vote on the legislation? You guessed it. He voted for labor law reform and against the position of his Committee's fund raising letters. By the way, as of June 1980, he had received over $32,000 from unions for his 1980 reelection to the Senate.

So as the Republican and Democratic parties avoided taking stands on controversial issues, citizens interested in those issues, out of their frustration and concern, banded together to make sure their views were represented.

Political parties have no one to blame but themselves for the breakdown and possible breakup of political parties.

Furthermore, both parties supported a law which made special interest groups all the more inevitable—the Federal Election Campaign Act of 1974. The act's intent was to get so-called "special interests" out of politics. But the result has been that single issue groups are into politics as they never were before the 1974 elections.

They have been significantly helped by the $1000 ceiling placed on the amount of money an individual may give to a candidate or committee. The new restriction forced candidates to find ways to finance elections outside the normal two-party structure.

Single issue groups sprang up and plunged into politics, writing letters, forming PACs, getting involved in campaigns. Millions of letters were written. Tens of millions of dollars were raised. Thousands of activists entered the political process.

Some candidates, instead of depending upon handouts from their national parties, put together their own large list of financial supporters, almost always through direct mail. Senator Jesse Helms showed how it could be done in his 1978 campaign when more than 190,000 people contributed nearly $7 million to his reelection. Those 190,000 contributors today give Jesse a financial and political base unsurpassed by any other Senator in American history. Consequently, the national Republican Party has next to no ability to influence Helms.

And thanks to the liberals and the national media who insisted on the passage of the 1974 election law, many Congressmen and Senators have 20,000, 30,000, 40,000 and some 50,000 and more individual contributors averaging $15 to $20 per contribution. As a result, the day of the traditional political boss issuing orders to Congressmen is gone in most parts of America.

The Jesse Helms operation in Raleigh, North Carolina has to be seen to be believed. Called The Congressional Club, it has seven departments, ranging from administration to advertising, a permanent staff of 40 (150 in an election year) and an annual budget that will hit $5 million in this election year of 1980.

The Club's honorary chairman and guiding spirit is Senator Helms. The chairman is Tom Ellis and the treasurer is Carter Wrenn—two of the most effective New Right leaders in America.

In 1980, The Congressional Club will help about 30 Congressional and Senatorial candidates as well as a number of state legislative candidates. It is also running an independent expenditure campaign for Ronald Reagan.

It has its own computer operation, its own mailing operation and its own printing shop.

The Congressional Club, in my opinion, is the first of many such New Right operations which will spring up around the country in the 1980's.

A sister operation is the Coalition for Freedom, an educational foundation, which distributes such films as "The Shining City on a Hill," featuring Senator Helms and Ronald Reagan.

I believe we need *more* not fewer single issue groups. As Senator Jake Garn of Utah put it at a New Right meeting in early 1979: "Political parties react to public pressure. Ten years ago, even five years ago, virtually all the public pressure was generated by the left. Today we're catching up, but we have a long way to go. We need more new and more effective groups."

Yes, we need ethnic groups. . . elderly groups . . . black middle class groups. . . blue collar groups. . . anti-busing groups. . . welfare reform groups. We need a group for every important issue in America so that the rights of the conservative majority in America will be adequately represented.

However, these groups would not be as necessary and certainly would not be as powerful as they are today if the Republican or Democratic party would effectively take up these single issues.

The second key to our success is the multi-issue group which is part of the conservative movement and makes no bones about it. Such a group is conservative first, last and always. It takes strong positions on every important conservative vs. liberal issue.

The multi-issue conservative movement group also takes a broad over-view of where we are going and the best way to get there.

It usually does not have as many members or supporters as single issue groups because its ranks are made up of individuals who are solidly conservative across the board.

The National Right to Work Committee can find over a million people who strongly oppose compulsory unionism.

The National Rifle Association can find nearly two million people who oppose federal gun registration.

Right to Life groups can find over a million people who oppose abortion.

But a conservative group which is pro-Right to Work, pro-Right to Life and pro-gun simply can't find a million contributors who agree on 20 different conservative issues.

For example, a local union leader may dislike the National Right to Work Committee but also oppose additional gun controls.

A pro-life supporter may not care one way or the other about compulsory unionism. And so forth.

But it is a sign of conservative strength that several of our broad spectrum groups do have, if not a million members, several hundred thousand.

Multi-issue broad spectrum groups such as The Conservative Caucus, the American Conservative Union, the Committee for the Survival of a Free Congress, the Heritage Foundation and the National Conservative Political Action Committee, to name but a few, are trying and succeeding in covering all the bases and all the issues for the conservative movement.

These movement groups are led by generalists like Paul Weyrich and Howard Phillips, who have well thought out positions on almost every issue. These groups are sensitive to all the elements of the growing conservative coalition. Their leaders can talk the language of all the single issue groups so vital to conservative growth.

When a Right to Work expert lectures at a Right to Life workshop on lobbying, it's a safe bet that a conservative movement leader had a hand in planning the workshop.

It is these leaders who work night and day to expand the leadership, educate each other in winning techniques and build ever larger and more influential coalitions.

I want to say something here about the internal dynamics of how we do things.

Some people think we are a big conspiracy. Others think we meet and vote on everything we do. Others think I give orders to everyone. These are all false ideas.

I have helped start a number of New Right groups, but I don't "control" any of them.

When we get together, we never vote on anything. Usually someone leads the discussion, but he has no more authority than anyone else present.

We exchange information. We brainstorm new ideas. Some people volunteer to do something or commit their organizations to do specific things. But no one gives orders like a commander-in-chief, or a Godfather.

Some gatherings are weekly, some twice a month, some annually, and so forth. But the majority are ad hoc.

We meet to work on special projects, say a piece of legislation. We meet as often as is necessary to do the best job we can for the conservative side of the issue.

We often bring in different leaders for different kinds of issues. We are creative in convincing different groups that their interests are the same as ours in particular battles.

That's how we got a broad spectrum of allies to fight instant voter registration, taxpayer campaign financing and other liberal election law power grabs.

Our informal way of operating is very frustrating to liberals who would love to have us tied up in formal organizations which would be easier to attack. But how do you use guilt by association against informal, ad hoc discussion groups?

Which brings me to the third part of the New Right's success — coalition politics.

Coalition politics is as old as the United States of America. You could call the original Thirteen Colonies a collection of issue groups who banded together to fight and defeat a common enemy — Great Britain.

The Republican Party was originally a coalition of issue groups — Free-Soil party members, pro-business northern Whigs, and some Democrats opposed to slavery.

FDR's New Deal was basically a coalition of groups — Southern farmers, blacks, Jews, organized labor, big city Democrats and the unemployed.

112

In fact, a liberal coalition based on the New Deal, the Fair Deal and the Great Society has dominated the nation for almost five decades.

But in the last 12 years, since Hubert Humphrey lost the Presidency to Richard Nixon in 1968, that coalition has begun to unravel. Conservatives didn't have the institutions to fill the gap then, but we do now.

Senator James McClure of Idaho has pointed out that conservative coalitions are forming in several different ways:

1. Outright Democrat-Republican coalitions in legislative leadership elections such as that of Robert Monier as president of the New Hampshire Senate. Monier proclaims: "We no longer have a minority party and a majority party. We have a majority coalition and a minority coalition."

2. Special group coalitions in elections such as the victories of Roger Jepsen in Iowa and Gordon Humphrey in New Hampshire, where supporters of Right to Life and Right to Work, gun owners, taxpayers, those favoring a strong national defense and others came together.

Such coalitions have also upset liberals in local races, like Helen Wise, former national chairman of the National Education Association union.

Mrs. Wise was elected a Pennsyvania state representative in 1976 with 62% of the vote. In 1978, despite the fact that her district includes the huge student population of Penn State University, Mrs. Wise was defeated by a young conservative attorney, Greg Cunningham, 51—49%.

At a subsequent Washington, D.C., meeting on the "threat" of the New Right, Mrs. Wise described herself as a "victim of some kind of right coalition." Because conservatives are coalescing, she said, there "aren't any more pure, single issues. And that's our problem." She listed the following issues as contributing to her defeat:

Taxes. Pennsylvania is a hyper-tax state, she said. She was astounded that her vote for "a tax which put 150 million dollars into the public schools of Pennsylvania" could be used against her in her university-dominated district.

Abortion. "It's going to be a force and you can't treat it in isolation," she warned, referring to the pro-life movement. Even in her "very liberal district," her pro-abortion votes generated fierce opposition. Wise reported that in her district, the most visible anti-abortionists "were not Catholics, they were fundamental religious groups."

Gun control. "I've never really taken a position" on the issue, Wise said. But she voted twice for the constitutional amendment which would almost certainly give D.C. two anti-gun liberal Democratic U.S. Senators and that, she said, cemented a coalition of sportsmen and rural Republicans which opposed her.

Right to Work. "An innocuous little bill which I voted for," she said, which would give some "meet and confer" powers sought by teachers' unions, made her a target of foes of compulsory unionism. Wise said that "more Right to Work material came out in our state in the last two years than ever before in its history."

Equal Rights Amendment. ERA, she said, "has not been an issue in Pennsylvania in seven or eight years." But she introduced a package of 26 bills to implement the state ERA. Then "all those who were vocally opposed to any kind of abortion or abortion choice, they suddenly also latched on the anti-ERAs, so they brought a few more people in."

Despite her analysis, Mrs. Wise revealed she didn't understand the conservative movement when she complained, "I was never accused of being immoral, just a lack of moral leadership, whatever that is."

In New York, the new Right-to-Life Party, led by Mary Jane Tobin, drew 130,000 votes in the November 1978 gubernatorial election, assuring itself the fourth place on the ballot for the next four years. In fifth place is the Liberal Party.

"It is essential," says Senator McClure, "that conservatives provide the leadership for those disaffected from the power structure or someone else will."

Coalition politics was being considered in the early 1970's by the Nixon White House. It was aimed at persuading Southern Democrats to change parties and thus take over the U.S. House of Representatives. But then Watergate came along, and coalitions fell victim to Nixon's problems as did a lot of other plans.

In the 1980's, the New Right is determined to do away with old-style politics.

In the past, liberals practiced coalition politics successfully while conservatives limited themselves to the Republican Party. No wonder we were such a small minority.

To put it bluntly, we were snookered. The liberals said what is ours is ours—the Democratic Party—and what is yours—the Republican Party—is negotiable.

So the liberals for many years have had almost 100% of the national Democratic Party and about 40% of the national Republican Party—giving the liberals about 70% of the political elections.

How can conservatives ever expect to govern if we concede 100% of the larger of the two major parties to the liberals without any fight and limit our fight to the political party which represents about 20% of the voters?

But the New Right is not willing to play by the liberals' rules. We are more than willing to support Democrats as long as they are Democrats who are basically right of center. It's a matter of simple arithmetic and common sense.

I want to make it clear that coalition politics does not necessarily mean a third party.

The impulse of some conservatives after Watergate (myself included) was to try to organize a brand new broadly based party, designed to replace the Republican Party. But the two-party system was, and is, probably too solidly entrenched for any such effort. It is a fact of life that Democratic and Republican politicians have written national and state laws in such a way that it's almost impossible to start a new political party.

Coalition politics includes working within the Republican and Democratic parties to nominate conservative candidates, promote conservative positions and create conservative majorities in both parties.

We must always be firm in putting principle before party. Some New Right leaders are established activists who fight for conservative principles within the Republican or Democratic

RAV and evangelist Jerry Falwell.

Viguerie Co. computer executives planning a mailing.
l to r: Mark O'Connor, Eddie Colbert, Ron Brooks, Andy Kuhrtz.

Ronald Reagan and RAV look over an issue of *Conservative Digest.*

Paul Brown, director of LAPAC, Mrs. Fob James (the wife of Alabama's governor) and Ed McAteer, chairman of The Religious Roundtable.

Congressmen Philip Crane and Jack Kemp on the U.S. Capitol steps.

Terry Dolan, Sen. Gordon Humphrey and Congressman Jerry Solomon on the trip to Taiwan.

Congressmen George Hansen and Lt. Gen. Daniel Graham, (USA) Ret. brief news media on Panama Canal Truth Squad objectives, February, 1978.

The Vigueries host a party at their home honoring Senator Hatch. l to r: Elaine Viguerie, Senator Hatch, RAV, Sue Edwards, Congressman Mickey Edwards.

Congressmen Norm Shumway, William Dannemeyer and Mickey Edwards and New Right leader Warren Richardson being briefed by Bill Rhatican on the way to Taiwan.

Sen. Barry Goldwater and Dan Popeo of the Washington Legal Foundation on their way to court to challenge President Carter's cancelling of the U.S.-Republic of China mutual defense treaty.

Holly Coors, Joseph Coors, Ed Feulner and Glenn Campbell, director of the Hoover Institution, at the dedication of the Holly and Joseph Coors Building of the Heritage Foundation.

Sen. James McClure, Howard Phillips and Sen. Jesse Helms at the Conservative Caucus 5th anniversary celebration.

Congressman Larry McDonald and Paul Weyrich on the Panama Canal Truth Squad plane.

l to r: Elaine's mother, Mrs. Adela O'Leary; Elaine's aunt, Mrs. Gertrude Cobb; RAV's mother, Elizabeth; Elaine Viguerie; and RAV's father, Arthur, at the elder Vigueries' home in Houston, Easter, 1974.

Milton Friedman, Ed Feulner and Rose Friedman at Heritage
headquarters in Washington.

British Prime Minister Margaret Thatcher and Right to Work
Committee President Reed Larson.

RAV, son Ryan, and daughters Renée and Michelle on a family outing, September, 1978.

RAV, actor Pat Boone and Congressman Robert Dornan at a Washington dinner honoring Boone.

RAV, Howard Phillips, William Rhatican and Congressman Mickey Edwards aboard the Panama Canal Truth Squad Plane.

Connaught Marshner, chairman, Library Court.

Congressman Robert Bauman and Mrs. Bauman.

Gregg Hilton, executive director, Conservative Victory Fund.

David Denholm, Public Service Research Council, John Laxalt, Citizens for the Republic, and Charlie Black, New Right leader.

RAV reviews advertising campaign with Viguerie Co. Vice Presidents Jim Aldigé, Ann Stone, Kathleen McDonald, Tom Kilpatrick and Jim Minarik.

Iowa Lt. Gov. Terry Branstad and Kathy Teague, ALEC executive director, at an ALEC meeting.

Bill Faulkner, Jerry Falwell and Dr. Bob Billings of the Moral Majority.

Margo Carlisle, Senate Steering Committee executive director, with Senators James McClure and Gordon Humphrey.

Paul Weyrich, CSFC director, and wife Joyce; RAV and Elaine; Sen. Paul Laxalt and wife Carol at a dinner when plaques were given Senator Laxalt and RAV for their successful efforts to stop taxpayer financing of Congressional elections.

Lee Edwards and William F. Buckley, Jr. backstage at a Washington conservative conference.

Conservatives throw a surprise 40th birthday party for Morton Blackwell. l to r: Mrs. Wm. G. Blackwell, Wm. G. Blackwell, Mrs. Charles Reddy, Morton Blackwell, Helen Blackwell, Richard Dingman, M. Stanton Evans.

parties. I used to think of myself as a Republican. Now I'm an Independent. And I have plenty of company. About 38% of the American electorate describe themselves as Independent.

Conservatives have the strength, the resources and the ability to operate in both major parties. In fact, because the Democratic Party is so much larger, there are many more conservative Democrats than conservative Republicans when you add up all the blue collar, ethnic, Catholic and other social conservative Democrats.

To sum it up, conservatives should neither abandon the Republicans nor ignore the Democrats.

We do not seek to eliminate the present political structures but to influence them to adopt the conservative point of view which we believe to be that of the majority of the American people.

Let me give you an example of the difference one conservative can make.

In February 1977, I wrote an article in *Conservative Digest* urging conservatives to get more active in the Democratic Party. Bob Perry, a Houston, Texas, home builder, read my column and persuaded a conservative Democrat to run against Congressman Bob Gammage in the Democratic Primary. The conservative Democrat got almost 44% of the vote and successfully identified Gammage (who spent about $100,000 in the primary) as a liberal in the minds of the voters.

In the fall, Republican Ron Paul, who had won and lost close contests against Gammage in previous Congressional elections, beat Gammage by about 2,000 votes. Without that conservative

challenge in the Democratic primary (which cost
Gammage both time and money that he couldn't
spend against Ron Paul), Gammage would almost
certainly have won.

In truth, the political parties have been so
weakened that in many areas they are like big
battleships without rudders or ammunition. The
time has come for conservatives to make the
effort needed to influence and, where possible,
provide direction for these powerful political
institutions.

Each party is a goldmine of opportunity.
Each has local, state and national committees,
Congressional campaign committees and Senatorial campaign committees as well as women's
groups, college groups and teenage groups. These
committees have important legal powers, huge
spending capabilities, easy access to news media
coverage and are often the key role in picking
who will be the party nominee.

And that is all important. As Tammany Hall
leaders said in the 19th century: Let us pick the
nominees. Then the people can elect whoever
they want in November.

Conservatives should work for the day when
the November election is between a conservative
Democrat and a conservative Republican. Then
we can go fishing or play golf on election day
knowing that it doesn't matter if a Republican
or Democrat wins—it's only important that a
conservative wins.

Probably about 80% of the November
elections for the past 30 years have been
between a liberal Democrat and a liberal Republican or a liberal Democrat and a conservative
Republican. And since only about 20% of the

voters consider themselves Republicans, how can conservatives, if they work only in the Republican party, come to power in the next five to ten years at the city, county, state and national level?

Occasionally, if the Democrats make enough mistakes and Republicans offer a strong candidate, we can win a Presidential race. But that's not governing America. Liberal Democrats or liberal Republicans will still control a majority of Congress, of the governors, of state legislatures, of the mayors, of county officials, etc.

State laws and party customs vary, but here are some of the specific powers of political party committees, as outlined by New Right analyst Morton Blackwell:

Elect party officers. . . control raising and spending of party funds. . . set dates, sites, rules and fees of party conventions which nominate or endorse candidates for public office. . .name new nominees when candidates die or withdraw before a general election. . . establish candidate recruitment procedures. . . control or strongly influence the election process of each state's delegates to national party conventions and members of national committees. . . pass resolutions on controversial public issues. . . endorse or condemn any public officeholder. . .provide valuable public forums for selected leaders or political candidates.

All of these powers can be summed up in one sentence: most of the political power in the United States is channeled through political party structures.

Right now, as you are reading this, there probably are vacancies on the party committees in the town or county where you live. Often you can get a seat immediately on a local party committee just by expressing your interest to the local party chairman. In other cases, you might have to wait a year or so before a new committee is elected in a primary or at a local party meeting.

Every political party has a crying need for volunteers. You will find that working a bit in your spare time on party projects will give you a leg up on most of the others who might want to serve on party committees.

There is a rapid turnover in most party leadership positions, which means a determined person can rise in the ranks very quickly. Liberals (and politicians with no philosophy) usually control party groups only by default. So very few people take part in party organizations that even a little input of conservative energy will work big changes quickly.

I want to talk now about the fourth reason for the New Right's success — direct mail.

Like all successful political movements, we must have a method of communicating with each other, and for conservatives in the 1970's it was direct mail.

Frankly, the conservative movement is where it is today because of direct mail. Without direct mail, there would be no effective counterforce to liberalism, and certainly there would be no New Right.

Some of the most common complaints I hear from conservatives are:

"I get too much mail." "I received six letters from one organization this month." "I get letters from twenty groups." "Why don't conservatives get together and form one organization?"

You may not have thought of it, but the U.S. mail is the principal method of communication for conservatives.

We sell our magazines, our books, and our candidates through the mail. We fight our legislative battles through the mail. We alert our supporters to upcoming battles through the mail. We find new recruits for the conservative movement through the mail.

Without the mail, most conservative activity would wither and die.

Most political observers agree that liberals have effective control of the mass media—a virtual monopoly on TV, radio, newspapers and magazines.

Walter Cronkite of CBS, Katherine Graham, head of the *Washington Post* and *Newsweek*, the heads of the *New York Times*, NBC, ABC, *Time*—to paraphrase Patrick Buchanan—draw up the agenda for the nation's public business. They determine who shall be heard and seen, what subjects shall be discussed, and for how long.

They decide that it's cost overruns in the military that is a major story and not cost overruns in the Welfare Department.

It's not that the media presents the news in a biased way, it's that they present the positive side of liberal causes, liberal issues, liberal personalities and, for the most part, ignore conservative causes, conservative issues and conservative personalities or present them in an unfavorable manner.

However, there is one method of mass commercial communication that the liberals do not control—direct mail. In fact, conservatives excel at direct mail.

There's an old saying that if a tree fell in a forest and no one was in the forest, it didn't make any noise.

Well, before conservatives started using direct mail in a major way, many of our good candidates, books, magazines, ideas, causes were unknown and ineffective because there was no method to tell the public about them—no one heard them.

Without direct mail, for example, President Ford would almost certainly have signed the common situs bill in January, 1976. But in the Fall of 1975, the National Right to Work Committee mailed over 4 million letters to people likely to agree with them on this issue. The mailings resulted in 720,000 letters and postcards to the White House, urging a presidential veto.

But without direct mail advertising, most conservatives would not have known that Ford was about to sign the bill. And even if they had heard about it, most would not have known what action to take.

The letters from the Right to Work Committee not only explained in detail how to write and where to send letters and post cards to Ford but also asked for a contribution to help pay for the cost of the direct mail advertising campaign.

Ford caved in and vetoed common situs which he had promised his secretary of labor, AFL-CIO head George Meany, and organized labor he would sign.

This same approach has been used many times by conservatives to help beat the Consumer Protection Agency, labor law reform, federal financing of Congressional elections, unionization of the military, SALT II, changes in the Hatch Act, etc., etc.

Congressmen Philip and Dan Crane of Illinois, George Hansen of Idaho, Robert Dornan of California, Bob Livingston of Louisiana, Mickey Edwards of Oklahoma and many other conservatives probably wouldn't be in Congress now if it weren't for national direct mail appeals for their campaigns.

In May 1980, I attended the dedication of the Joseph and Holly Coors and Edward Noble Buildings of the Heritage Foundation in Washington, D.C. Each building was made possible by a very generous contribution of these three people—and by direct mail.

Without Heritage's 100,000 plus small contributors, it would be limited as to what it could receive from large donors, either individual, corporate or foundation.

Without direct mail, we might have no *National Review*, no *Human Events*, no *Conservative Digest*, no conservative PACs, no effective organizations in Right to Work, Right to Life, pro-gun, anti-busing, national defense, pro-family, no large national conservative organizations and youth training.

You can think of direct mail as *our* TV, radio, daily newspaper and weekly newsmagazine.

Some people persist in thinking of direct mail as only fund raising. But it's really mostly advertising.

Raising money is only one of several purposes of direct-mail advertising letters. A letter may ask you to vote for a candidate, volunteer for campaign work, circulate a petition among your neighbors, write letters and postcards to your Senators and Congressmen, urging them to pass or defeat legislation and also ask you for money to pay for the direct mail advertising campaign.

Direct mail is, in fact, the third largest form of advertising in the country, spending about $7.3 billion in 1978, third only to television and newspapers.

"Junk mail," by the way, is a phrase probably first used by the Scripps-Howard newspapers in the 1940's. I can understand why they did it. After all, direct mail was then the number one competitor of newspapers for the advertising dollar.

It is a unique form of advertising. If done properly, it pays for itself which is something almost no other form of advertising can do for conservatives.

It is the advertising medium of the underdog. It allows organizations or causes not part of the mainstream or not popular to get funding.

Direct mail is the advertising medium of the non-establishment candidate.

Sometimes the giants of TV and radio make decisions, for whatever reason, that stifle free speech.

For example, the three major TV networks, ABC, NBC and CBS, established a policy of not selling time to any political candidate in 1979.

That decision may not hurt you if you are the President of the U.S. with all of the power that goes with the office. But if you are Senator Kennedy, it can keep your campaign from getting off to a proper start.

And again, the networks' decision may not be a serious problem if you are the front runner in the G.O.P. with 35% support, as Ronald Reagan was in the summer of 1979. But it can be a devastating blow if you are John Connally with 10% support and want to get on TV to promote your candidacy.

The three major networks seriously damaged John Connally's ability to win the Republican nomination by keeping him off TV in 1979.

George McGovern became the Democratic Presidential nominee in 1972 because of direct mail.

Through direct mail, McGovern found about 250,000 supporters who financed his race. From this list of 250,000, McGovern's field organizers were given the names of individuals which were used in organizing for primaries and caucuses.

When he couldn't afford to advertise on television, McGovern could spend $200,000 (mostly on credit) to write to 1 million identified liberal Democrats, knowing that an appeal for money in the letters would bring in enough funds within 30 days to pay for the direct mail advertising.

So George McGovern and his brilliant direct mail team of Morris Dees and Tom Collins used the mails to bypass the party bosses, the party establishment, and the smoke-filled rooms to go straight to the people.

Most of the news media didn't understand political direct mail, until George McGovern came along that year and made it an acceptable political tool.

Independent Presidential candidate John Anderson is depending heavily on direct mail. In the first part of 1980, his direct mail expert Roger Craver was mailing to his house file (those who have already given to Anderson) about once every eight days.

In fact, I feel confident that John Anderson would not have been a serious candidate for President in 1980 without David Garth and Roger Craver. While most politically knowledgeable people have heard of Garth, an outstanding TV and political expert, very few have heard of Craver.

But without Craver, John Anderson would not have had the money to travel around the country (and to Europe and the Middle East in July) and buy TV and radio ads. He would have been just another minor candidate who never caught fire.

In the first seven months of 1980, Craver mailed 7 million letters, developed a list of 157,600 contributors, and raised $7 million through direct mail for John Anderson.

George McGovern, John Anderson, Jesse Helms—they all understand that direct mail is basically an advertising medium. And they understand that repetition is absolutely necessary.

If you see three ads for Coca Cola in one day, you don't get upset or think the Coke people are wasting their money. If you are a Ford Motor Co. stockholder and you see five ads for Ford cars in one week, you don't get upset and think that they are wasting your money.

It's the same way with direct mail. By the way, to the best of my knowledge, in no other country do people give money to political causes through the mails as we do in America.

Look at what happened to Congressman Phil Crane. He took a $15,000 investment in the summer of 1978 and by using direct mail became a well-known political figure.

With that $15,000 (a personal loan to his Presidential committee), he was able to raise more than $5 million (including about $2 million matching money from the government) with which he promoted conservative ideas, compiled a list of 80,000 contributors, and aimed his candidacy for President at those Republicans likely to vote in GOP primaries.

Direct mail was the only advertising medium that made sense for Phil Crane.

I want to say just a few words about the cost of direct mail. First of all, the organization that profits the most from mailing is the U.S. Post Office. Out of every dollar spent on direct mail, about 35 to 40 cents goes for postage.

Then there are the costs of printing the letter, the brochure and other enclosures, plus the envelopes. You also have to pay the mailing house, mailing list owner, and the advertising agency which creates and coordinates the entire package.

It is not a cheap medium, but it is a highly effective one if you know what you're doing. And conservatives do. That's why the liberals are always screaming about direct mail and trying to figure out ways—like cutting the amount of money PACs can give to a candidate, preventing Congressmen and Senators from using exact reproductions of their official stationery for letters helping non-profit organizations, and public financing of Congressional campaigns—to make direct mail less effective for us.

Where would conservatives be without direct mail? We would be where we were 20 years ago, on the defensive, isolated, fighting losing battles.

Some years back, a few of my fellow conservatives were critical of me. They said I was mailing too much and that I should not help new organizations get started. They took the approach that the conservative resources were like a pie to be divided among several organizations. They were worried about more groups cutting it into thinner and thinner slices. They feared that their own organizations would get smaller slices of the conservative money pie.

I rejected that philosophy. I felt that if we only had about 100,000 potential conservative contributors in the nation, we were wasting our time trying to beat the liberals. I knew you couldn't turn the country around with only 100,000 contributors.

I felt there were millions of Americans who would contribute if asked. So I and others set out to find and identify millions of new conservative contributors and supporters. We found them, I'm happy to say. The Viguerie Co. now has some 4½ million people we can identify as having indicated an interest in a conservative candidate or cause over the last four years. I think we can add at least another 4 million in the next three years.

There is another key to New Right success—our positive attitude toward the news media.

From the time I started in politics in the mid 1950's until the early 1970's, most conservatives and the national media were like cats and dogs, or oil and water — they just didn't mix.

Then in the early 1970's some of the national media began to notice our political activities.

I have to be honest and say that I shared the traditional conservatives' position on the press. Which was avoid them, recognize that they are all liberals, and be convinced that their basic purpose is to attack conservatives.

I remember one day a fairly well known writer for a major newspaper called and wanted an appointment to come and talk to me.

I was a little short of terrified. I told my secretary that we'd get back to him.

I then called some of my conservative associates and asked what I should do. Almost all advised me to avoid the reporter.

The advice went something like this - that newspaper is no friend of the conservative movement, that reporter will try to do you in, etc., etc.

But then I got to thinking. I and my conservative friends are not playing in the big leagues — but we want to.

We're not having a major influence on national policies — but we want to.

We're not close to our goal of governing America — but we want to.

I called the reporter back and said, "Why don't you come over and, if you've got time, why don't we go to lunch?"

Well, I spent an enjoyable three hours with the reporter. He wrote a basically fair and accurate story (although it wasn't as fair and objective as my mother would have written.)

And from that day forward, I felt that I and other conservatives had to change our view of the press.

I can think of no better example of the difference between the New Right and the old right.

We realize that reporters and editors are not monsters, or even hopeless ideologues.

The vast majority are good, decent men and women who are trying to do a professional job and are looking for the kind of news which will put their stories on the front page or the nightly TV newscasts.

During the next few years, the New Right's relationship with the press improved. We felt comfortable with the press and they began to cover our activities.

However, in the spring of 1977 I realized that my associates in the New Right and I needed a more professional approach to the media.

We were dealing with the media in a casual, almost accidental way. We needed someone to introduce us to the major media, to teach us how to call and conduct a press conference, how to have a press breakfast, how to get our thoughts across in a few seconds on TV, how to hold activities that the press would be interested in covering.

So in April 1977, Bill Rhatican came into the New Right's life.

Bill had been press secretary to Treasury Secretary Bill Simon and Interior Secretary Rogers Morton and a top aid to Ron Nessen in the Ford White House.

I hired Bill to be vice president of public affairs at The Viguerie Co. The vast majority of his time was spent with the clients of The Viguerie Co. He immediately threw himself heavily into key battles then being waged by the New Right — the Panama Canal, instant voter registration and taxpayer financing of Congressional Elections.

And another big step forward was taken by the New Right.

Single issue groups — multi-issue groups — coalition politics — direct mail — these have been the four cornerstones of conservative growth and success in the 1970's. They will help us build a new majority in America in the 1980's.

As Congressman Newt Gingrich of Georgia has put it: "The way you build a majority in this country is you go out and put together everybody who's against the guy who's in. And instead of asking the question, What divides us?, you ask the question, What unites us?"

And what unites most conservatives, Republican, Democratic and Independent, is a desire for less government and more freedom for every American.

VII

Our Goal:
Military Superiority

Maybe once in a lifetime is there a chance to turn around the politics of America. We are at such a turning point right now—made possible by the collapse of America's military defenses under 20 years of liberal Presidents and Congresses.

How bad off are we?

By all standards—overall spending, strategic air weapons, naval forces, ground forces—we have fallen far behind the Soviets.

• In military manpower, Soviet Russia has armed forces of 4 million. We have about 2 million men and women, all volunteer.

• They have close to 50,000 tanks, we have 10,500. They have about 20,000 field artillery, we have some 6,000.

• The Soviets have an estimated 3,736 strategic offensive weapons, including ICBMs, SLBMs, cruise missiles and manned bombers. We have 2,124 such offensive weapons.

- They have 14,664 strategic defensive weapons, including SAMs and fighter planes. We have 309, repeat, 309 such defensive weapons.
- The Soviets have 594 major ships and submarines. We have 296 such vessels.
- Since the early 1970's, Soviet Russia has been spending three times as much as the U.S. on strategic weapons alone.
- In 1978, the Defense Nuclear Agency estimated that Soviet Russia was ahead of the United States in 33 of 41 categories of strategic power.

Clearly, we have fallen from being the Number One military power in the world to the Number Two power—behind a country whose leaders are totally committed to defeating America and conquering the world.

The Soviets have not tried to hide their goal.

"We are achieving with detente what our predecessors have been unable to achieve using the mailed fist. . . (By 1985) we will have consolidated our position. We will have improved our economy. And a decisive shift in the correlation of forces will be such that, come 1985, we will be able to exert our will whenever we need to."

—Leonid Brezhnev (1973 in East Germany)

"Our aim is to gain control of the two great houses on which the West depends—the energy treasure house of the Persian Gulf and the mineral treasure house of central and southern Africa."

—Leonid Brezhnev
(to then Somali President Siad Barre)

"We will bury you."
—Nikita Khrushchev (Moscow, 1956)

Liberal presidents and liberal Congresses have deliberately put us in second place, believing that America's overwhelming strength was a threat to the Soviets and world peace.

In *The Eleventh Hour*, General Lewis W. Walt former commandant of the U.S. Marine Corps, explains how it happened:

"The triad of weapons which provided us with a shield against both nuclear war and nuclear blackmail was based on land-based missiles, submarine-launched missiles and strategic bombers. . .

"(But) our strategic triad has aged and lost its ability to deter war.

"The president and a majority in congress have refused to replace the B-52 (bomber), designed in 1948; they have delayed building a mobile missile system; they have scrapped our air defense and civil defense; they have delayed the neutron warhead; and they have frozen the third leg of the triad, the nuclear subs, by diplomatic agreement."

In 1965, Defense Secretary Robert McNamara established this disarmament policy when he declared: "The Soviets have decided that they have lost the quantitative race. . . there is no indication the Soviets are seeking to develop a strategic nuclear force as large as ours."

Such dangerous misjudgments by the liberals have resulted in unilateral disarmament by America while the Soviets have forged ahead of us in every military category. Liberals, in effect, have issued an open invitation to increased Soviet aggression around the world.

Russia invades Afghanistan and we react by stopping the future sale of wheat to them, which they turn around and buy from Argentina.

Cuban troops, trained and armed by the Russians, occupy South Yemen, Angola, Ethiopia, and other African nations. Our feeble response is to ask the United Nations for a resolution condemning such aggression.

The basic problem is that the United States is engaged in a worldwide war with Communism, but most liberals refuse to believe that the Communists are really working to conquer the world. In the 1930's most leaders in democratic countries (with a few exceptions like Winston Churchill and Douglas MacArthur) refused to believe that the Germans and the Japanese had any intention of conquering the world. Yet Hilter explained his plans in detail in his book, *Mein Kampf*, published in 1925.

European leaders ignored Hitler until too late. As a result, more than 25 million babies, children, women and men paid with their lives and hundreds of millions more suffered through the death and serious injury of their loved ones or the destruction of their homes and property during Hitler's war in Europe.

The major Communist leaders have written hundreds of books, and made millions of speeches declaring their ultimate goal of completely destroying capitalism and freedom. Yet, the vast majority of the leaders of the free world (most of them liberals) still refuse to believe the Communists.

Maybe I could understand why the liberals refuse to believe conservatives, but this question demands an answer:

Given the 63-year record of the Communists, why do so many liberals still refuse to believe those farther left on the political spectrum—the Communists?

Consider the Communists' own words:

"We stand for permanent revolution."

—V. Lenin

"As long as capitalism and socialism exist, we cannot live in peace: in the end, one or the other will triumph—a funeral dirge will be sung either over the Soviet Republic or over world capitalism."

—V. Lenin

"I can prophesy that your grandchildren in America will live under socialism."

—N. Khrushchev

"Can the capitalists be forced out and the roots of capitalism be annihilated without a bitter class struggle? No, it is impossible."

—Joseph Stalin

"Every Communist must grasp that political power grows out of the barrel of a gun. . . In fact, we can say that the whole world can be remolded only with a gun."

—Mao Tse-tung

Consider the Communists' 63-year record of conquest:

• In 1917, they seized control of Tsarist Russia.

- In 1920, they took over the non-Russian nations of Armenia, Azerbaijan, Byelorussia, Cossackia, Udel-Ural, North Caucasia, Georgia and Ukraine—the last two of which they had earlier recognized as independent countries.
- In 1922, they absorbed the Far Eastern Republic and Turkestan.
- In 1924, they seized the Mongolian People's Republic.
- In 1940, they invaded and absorbed the Baltic States—Estonia, Latvia and Lithuania.
- In 1946, they seized Albania, Bulgaria, and Yugoslavia (including Serbia, Croatia, Slovenia, etc.).
- In 1948, they seized Czechoslovakia and North Korea.
- In 1949, they took over Hungary, East Germany and the biggest nation of all—Mainland China.
- In 1951, they absorbed Tibet.
- In 1954, they took over North Vietnam.
- In 1959, they seized Cuba.

Consider the Communists' record of conquest over the last five years:
- In 1974-75, they seized control of Ethiopia, black Africa's oldest state.
- In 1975, they gained South Vietnam and Cambodia.
- In 1976, they took over Angola and Mozambique.
- In 1977, they seized Laos.
- In 1978, they seized South Yemen.
- In 1979, they invaded and took over Afghanistan.

Consider the human cost of Communism.

British journalist D. G. Stewart-Smith, in his book *Defeat of Communism*, estimated that from 1917 to 1964, international Communism was directly responsible for the death of 83 million people—excluding World War II. More than 45 million deaths were in Soviet Russia through civil war, famines, purges, slave labor camps and the "liquidation" of the peasant farmers.

As I have stated elsewhere, American expert Richard Walker has estimated in an official document for the U.S. Senate that at least 32 million and possibly as many as 62 million Chinese died as a result of Communism in China.

Alexander Solzhenitsyn has eloquently described the human cost of Communism in the Soviet slave camps in his epic, *The Gulag Archipelago*.

In his definitive work, *Workers Paradise Lost*, Eugene Lyons wrote that "no fewer than 50 million Soviet citizens" lived and usually died in Soviet labor camps.

In view of the Communists' bloody record and in view of the liberals' apparent inability to acknowledge it, I can't help but wonder:

Do the liberals really deserve their reputation of having great compassion and concern for their fellow men?

• It is liberals who have urged a policy of disarmament which has made the U.S. Number Two to the Soviet Union in military strength.

• It is liberals who have pushed a policy of detente which has allowed the Communists to expand their power and influence in Africa,

139

Central America, the Middle East and the Far East.

• It is liberals with their double standard regarding human rights who have magnified scattered violations in anti-Communist nations like Chile and Taiwan while downplaying massive oppression in Soviet Russia and Communist China.

• It is liberals who refuse to accept the fact, stated so openly by Nikita Khrushchev and succeeding Communist leaders, that Communism is "out to bury" the Free World.

To put it bluntly, we are locked in world-wide combat with Communism. In fact, as British strategic expert Brian Crozier has written, we have been fighting the Third World War since before the Second World War ended.

Yes, even before the end of the fighting in Europe and the Pacific, Joseph Stalin was laying plans for Communist domination of his neighbors. The Soviet armies that pursued the retreating Nazis into Eastern Europe stayed and imposed Communism on the peoples of Poland, Hungary, Czechoslovakia, Yugoslavia, Rumania, Bulgaria, Albania and East Germany.

Stalin later commented: " The reason why there is now no Communist government in Paris is because in the circumstance of 1945 the Soviet Army was not able to reach French soil."

For the last third of a century, the Communists have continued to wage war while the Free World has followed a policy of so-called "containment" which has failed.

In the last 63 years more than 1.8 billion men, women and children have been taken, not by their choice, behind the ever-expanding Iron, Bamboo and Sugar Cane Curtains.

The Communists never fail to take advantage of every crisis situation. We seem to spend most of our time creating crisis situations—as in Iran.

When the Shah of Iran was ousted in early 1979, the Carter administration determined to show the world that American power had not disappeared.

So Carter sent an aircraft carrier steaming in circles in the South China Sea.

Carter sent unarmed airplanes to Saudi Arabia.

Carter remained silent when U.N. Ambassador Andrew Young said of the Shah's successor, the Ayatollah Khomeini, "He might be a saint."

Carter sent an ultra-liberal apostle of appeasement, Ramsey Clark, in a vain attempt to meet with the Ayatollah.

Carter did everything but what he should have done—stick by the Shah, our ally for 37 years, so that he could continue to help stabilize the Middle East.

The Soviet Union once again showed everyone but liberals their true intentions (world conquest) by invading Afghanistan and turning it into another Soviet colony.

Within one week of the Soviet invasion of Afghanistan, the Carter administration warned them to stop. The Soviets responded by sending 15,000 more troops into Afghanistan.

Jimmy Carter did call for a boycott of the Moscow Olympics. But he failed, as usual, to put enough pressure on our major allies to follow our example. He was unable to lead, once again.

That's why I have called for a boycott of products made in France, Italy, and Eastern

European countries such as East Germany, Poland and Czechoslovakia not supporting our boycott of the Olympics.

The Olympics are now over, but I think we should let France and other nations know how angry we are about their failure to stand with us on a critical issue like the invasion of Afghanistan.

I believe that it is the responsibility of all freedom-loving people to help other people who are being murdered and enslaved.

Our boycott can make a difference. You and I can help provide the leadership America so desperately needs.

I can remember back in the 1960's that conservative groups like Young Americans for Freedom were able to get Firestone not to trade with the Communists through picket lines and other action projects. I think it's time once again to use the boycott and similar tactics against any nation which is not on our side in the continuing struggle against Communism.

Frustrated by its continuing failure to free the American hostages in Teheran, the Carter administration begged the United Nations to adopt economic sanctions against Iran. But most of our allies have refused to impose the sanctions across the board, making them almost meaningless.

America has indeed become, in the words of former President Richard Nixon, "a pitiful helpless giant."

But it was Nixon and former Secretary of State Henry Kissinger who were responsible for the policy of detente which helped make us pitiful and helpless.

And detente prepared the way for Jimmy Carter's incredible 1977 speech at Notre Dame when he declared that America had entered "a new world" freed from "that inordinate fear of Communism" which led three U. S. Presidents into the "moral poverty" of Vietnam.

Carter revealed his true liberal bent by stopping the B—1 bomber. . . sending a U. S. diplomatic mission to Cuba. . . promising to abide by SALT II, even if the Senate refused to ratify it. . . trying to remove U. S. ground troops from South Korea. . . supporting the Soviet-backed Patriotic Front in Rhodesia. . . denouncing small right-wing countries such as South Africa and Chile for alleged violations of human rights but ignoring massive murder and oppression of human beings in left-wing countries such as Cuba, Vietnam, Communist China and Soviet Russia.

The Soviet invasion of Afghanistan did shake up Jimmy Carter, causing him to say on December 31, 1979: "My opinion of the Russians has changed more drastically in the last week than even the previous 2½ years before that."

You can't help but wonder as columnist George Will wrote a week later: "How serious is change brought on by a 55-year-old man suddenly noticing a 62-year-old reality, the nature of Soviet statecraft?"

But within a few weeks, Carter showed his true liberal self by insisting that SALT II was still needed. And he has been far less than candid about the so-called halting of U.S. exports to Russia because of Afghanistan.

According to Lawrence Brady, deputy director of the U. S. Office of Export Administration, Department of Commerce, from 1974-

79, the Carter embargo affected only 7% of our exports to the Soviet Union.

Untouched for example was a diesel engine assembly line made by Ingersoll-Rand which was to go to the Soviet Kama River plant, the largest truck plant in the world (which, by the way, was built by American big business).

A number of these trucks are outfitted for use as missile carriers, armed personnel carriers and command vehicles. And it has been reliably reported that Soviet armed personnel carriers made at Kama River are being used to crush freedom fighters in Afghanistan.

You have to ask yourself, "Would engines made on this Ingersoll-Rand assembly line be used in future Afghanistans?" And your answer has to be, as Carter used to say, "You can depend on it."

However, Brady's exposure of this assembly line deal put increasing heat on the U.S. Department of Commerce. Finally, in mid-1980, it began to take steps which may well stop shipment of this high technology assembly line to the Soviets.

For his honesty and integrity, Brady was forced out of his government job by the Department of Commerce, despite protests by the Merit Systems Protection Board, a federal commission set up to protect whistle-blowers.

Brady's expose was the latest of many exposes resulting from the Nixon-Kissinger-Carter doctrine of detente. Here are a few more examples of how American businessmen have sold strategic equipment which the Soviets have used to build up their war machine.

• *Precision grinders.* In 1972, the Soviets obtained 164 Centalign-B ball-bearing grinder machines, manufactured by the Bryant Chucking Grinder Company. Four years later, Defense Intelligence Agency officials told Congress that the grinders "may now be used in the guidance equipment of Soviet missiles."

• *Oil drilling technology.* In the fall of 1978, the Carter administration approved 74 export licenses, including a $144 million oil drill bit factory by Dresser Industries. The sale involved the transfer of an electronic beam welding machine that can be used to make jet aircraft and might also have nuclear and laser applications.

• *Computers.* U. S. computer sales to the Soviet Union have run into hundreds of millions of dollars. Dr. Miles Costick, a leading defense analyst and author, has noted that the export of American computers, including the Control Data Cyber 73 and the IBM 370/145, 370/155 and 370/158 to Moscow "will enhance Soviet strategic capabilities across the board."

In 1977, then FBI Director Clarence Kelley told an industrial association that "businessmen who sell technology to the Soviet bloc are making a tragic mistake." He pleaded with U.S. businessmen to put "patriotism over profit, knowledge over naivete."

But it appears that many big businessmen don't care what happens tomorrow as long as they make a sale today.

I'd like to say something here about the so-called "love affair" between the conservative movement and big business. As far as the New Right is concerned, it never existed.

It is not true that what is good for General Motors is necessarily good for the country and

145

what is good for big business is automatically good for conservatives.

The truth is that big business has become far too cozy with big government. In fact, big government protects big business. It's a sweetheart arrangement. Big business is comfortable with red tape, regulations, bureaucracy—it holds down competition.

We've seen so-called believers in "free enterprise" like Lockheed and Chrysler run crying to Congress for bailouts because they made bad business decisions.

We've seen business and association PACs make sizeable financial contributions to incumbent liberal Congressmen while ignoring promising conservative challengers.

We've seen big business spend millions of dollars on advertising in pornographic publications like *Hustler* and *Penthouse* without any regard for the impact of these publications on our greatest natural resource—our young people.

Big business can no longer take the support of conservatives for granted. In the future, they must earn it and they have a lot of changing to do before they get it.

Especially in the area of trading with our enemy—the Communists.

Lenin was correct when he reportedly said that capitalists would sell the Communists the rope to hang themselves.

In fact, most of the Communist countries pay for products bought from American corporations by credit. But the American big businessman takes almost no risk because the Communist credit is guaranteed by the American government.

That means that you the taxpayer are making it possible for big American corporations to make a profit selling truck factories, computers and oil drilling equipment to the Communists—just as they did in the 1930's when American corporations sold scrap iron to Japan that was later used to kill Americans in World War II.

The alarming surge in Communist debt to Western countries and banks since the start of detente is a serious problem for the Free World.

By the end of 1979, the Soviet bloc owed an estimated $75 billion to Western governments and banks—up from $17.6 billion in 1973.

There is real doubt about the Communists' ability or intention to repay their debts. And the size of their debt gives the Communists enormous power. There's an old saying: "Make a small loan and you have a debtor; make a large loan and you have created a partner."

For an example of the danger of large loans, look at how U.S. bankers lobbied strongly for the Panama Canal treaties. Could it have been because of Panama's $2.4 billion dollar debt to the bankers?

And Moscow's black record of consistently breaking treaties make the chances of its repaying its financial debts very questionable.

V. I. Lenin is the final authority for all good Communists on how to conduct themselves. Here is what Lenin said in 1918 about agreements: "It is ridiculous not to know that a treaty is a means of gaining strength."

While Stalin, his successor for 29 years, said about diplomatic lying: "A diplomat's words must have no relation to action—otherwise, what kind of diplomacy is it?

147

"Words are one thing, actions another. Good words are a mask for the concealment of bad deeds. Sincere diplomacy is no more possible than dry water or iron wood."

Dr. Igor Glagolev, a member of the Soviet negotiating team for SALT who defected to the United States, has described the Russians' real intentions this way:

"In the period of the talks on SALT I (signed in 1972), the Brezhnev-Andropov leadership of the USSR took the following decisions:

"—to achieve an overwhelming military superiority over the United States, a superiority sufficient to win not only conventional wars in different parts of the world but also an all-out nuclear war;

"—to conceal this superiority from the public with the help of the censorship in the USSR and the pro-Soviet media in the West;

"—to establish Soviet influence in Indochina and Africa with the help of local Communist or pro-Communist forces organized and armed by the Soviet Union;

"—to break the agreement on peace in Vietnam and the Helsinki agreements."

Can anyone deny that this is precisely and exactly what the Soviets have done in the last eight years?

Yet the Third World War is not over. It can still be won by the Free World if we take certain critical steps without delay.

The first and most important is to abandon detente which has been a disaster for the West. Dr. Paul Eidelberg, an American foreign policy analyst, has outlined just how disastrous in his remarkable book, *Beyond Detente: Toward An*

American Foreign Policy. According to Dr. Eidelberg, the consequences of detente are:

• It dignifies the rulers of the Soviet Union, increasing their domestic and international prestige and power.

• It discourages internal resistance in the Soviet Union among the intellectuals and the people.

• It undermines freedom movements in the satellites.

• It places the stamp of legitimacy on Soviet domination of Eastern Europe, prolonging Communist oppression of hundreds of millions.

• It enables Moscow to divide and undermine NATO, especially by means of bilateral agreements with individual members of the Western alliance.

• It makes easier Soviet espionage in the U. S., economic as well as military.

• It renders Communist propaganda more effective by silencing criticism of the Soviet regime.

• It weakens the will to resist Communism by discouraging anti-communism.

• It lulls the Free World into complacency, leading to reduction in defense expenditures.

Detente, Dr. Eidelberg argues and I agree, is not a policy of peace but one of appeasement which increases the likelihood of nuclear war.

In place of detente we need a policy of military superiority over the Communists (history shows that superior military strength is the best way to prevent war with an aggressor country) combined with a multi-billion dollar effort to fight the Communists with propaganda in every country of the world.

As George Washington said, "The best way to insure peace is to be prepared for war."

A number of leading conservative experts, including Dr. Eidelberg, General Daniel Graham, Brian Crozier of London, Congressman Jack Kemp and General Lewis A. Walt, have proposed in their books and articles what might be called a victory policy. No, these distinguished authorities do not recommend a nuclear attack on the Soviet Union. But they do urge that the United States and the Free World adopt a political, economic, diplomatic *offensive* against Communism.

Here is a summary of major conservative proposals on foreign policy and national defense:

• Regain strategic military superiority without delay.

• Stop any technology, capital investments or loans which could advance, directly or indirectly, the war-making power of the Soviet Union.

• Expose and condemn Soviet violations of international agreements and laws.

• Develop the conventional military power necessary to respond to the various kinds of Soviet-supported aggression.

• Use diplomatic devices like recalling our ambassador and severing diplomatic relations when the Soviets use force against their satellites or other nations as they did to Czechoslovakia in 1968 and Afghanistan in 1979.

• Free America from arms control restraints which perpetuate U. S. military inferiority and force us to fight the Third World War by Soviet rules.

Anthony Dolan, winner of a Pulitzer Prize for journalism in 1978 and a special assistant to campaign director William Casey in the Reagan Presidential effort, suggested some foreign policy initiatives in *National Review* in May 1980. They dealt with Soviet weakness in an important but frequently neglected area—captive nations. Dolan proposed:

• The U. S. ambassador to the United Nations bring before the General Assembly a demand for the removal of the Soviet occupation forces in Eastern Europe as well as Afghanistan. The ambassador would back up his demand with the facts about Soviet invasion and suppression for over 30 years of the peoples of Hungary, Czechoslovakia, Poland, etc.

• The White House would announce a new form of "linkage"—including in any future diplomatic negotiations with Moscow the demand for Soviet withdrawal from Eastern Europe.

• A call for troop removal and free elections not only in Eastern Europe but the Baltic nations of Latvia, Estonia and Lithuania and the non-Russian republics of Ukraine, Georgia, Turkistan and so forth.

Such demands, as Dolan pointed out, would focus UN debates not on "absurd discussions of colonialism in the Virgin Islands and Puerto Rico" but on the critical issue of this century— Soviet Russian imperialism.

We should also:

• Increase and expand anti-Communist propaganda and information, with special attention focused on Radio Free Europe and Radio Liberty.

151

Dr. Fred Schwarz argues that with 1% of the U.S. military budget, about $1.4 billion, propaganda "miracles could be wrought." An "army of authors and translators," in Dr. Schwarz' words, could be recruited and set to work producing material about the doctrines, history and objectives of Communism.

Printing companies could produce literature in every language designed for every segment of the world's population. Messages could be produced for radio broadcast. Films could be made and distributed to every corner of the world.

Says Dr. Schwarz: "The change in the world scene would be dramatic. The advance of communism would stop."

We should also:

• Rebuild our security and intelligence-gathering capability. We need the Defense Intelligence Agency, the CIA and the National Security Agency abroad and the FBI at home to let us know what our enemies are doing.

For example, there was a 99% drop in domestic security cases in the mid-70's, from 21,414 to just 214 in 1977. Meanwhile, 1,900 registered Soviet bloc officials went about their spy business and thousands of potential terrorists (as reported in *Conservative Digest* in October 1977) prepared for their next bombing or kidnapping.

We should also:

• Strengthen U. S. alliances, particularly friends and allies not only in Western Europe but in Latin America, southern Africa and Asia.

• Support pro-Western forces under Soviet-sponsored attack. We helped preserve the peace in Europe, the Middle East and North-eastern Africa in the 1940's and 1950's. Our recent record has been far less impressive, as Congressman Kemp says, in Angola, Mozambique, Ethiopia and Southeast Asia.

• Accept the heavy burden of international leadership. As Brian Crozier has warned, "Unless a new awareness and alertness are fostered, and unless the right action is taken in time, then the way of life that is under threat is indeed doomed—not by any law of 'historical inevitability' as the Marxist might suppose, but by internal demoralization and a loss of will to face the threats from without and within."

"A loss of will." How often that phrase is used by conservative experts as they analyze why the Free World has failed to meet the challenge of Communism. The ability to act counts for little unless it is accompanied by the willingness to act.

And always there is the element of time. Before 1963, it took about six years to translate an idea into a weapons system. Now it takes an estimated 15 years. In other words, the MX missile, a needed counterforce weapon, will not be ready for another 10 years if we proceed at our present pace.

I believe we must return to a World War II emergency method of rebuilding our military position. That would mean doing away with time-consuming purchasing requirements, arms control impact statements, low bids, and any EPA or OSHA rules that hampered production. It would mean keeping some plants open 24 hours a day. It would mean a total commitment by everyone from the President to the worker on the job and a realization that we are at war with a dangerous enemy.

In the early 1940's when we had to build an arsenal or watch Germany and Japan conquer the world, the United States amazed friend and foe alike by setting production records never seen before or since. From 1940 through 1945, according to historian William Manchester, America turned out:

- 296,429 warplanes.
- 102,351 tanks.
- 372,431 artillery pieces.
- 2,455,964 trucks.
- 87,620 warships.
- 5,425 cargo ships.
- 5,822,000 tons of aircraft bombs.
- 20,986,061 small arms.
- 44 billion rounds of small arms ammunition.

As the old song goes, "We did it before and we can do it again." But today, we have much less time.

The alternative to such an all-out all-American effort is simple. The Soviets will either force us into a war we will lose or we will be forced to surrender.

VIII

The Born-Again
Christian Discovers Politics

When Jimmy Carter campaigned for President in 1976, he put together a coalition (much as Franklin D. Roosevelt did 44 years earlier) of widely different groups: union officials, blacks, McGovern activists, environmentalists, Naderites and fundamentalist Christians.

Carter had been elected only a few hours when most of these groups were bragging loudly how their support had made the difference between winning and losing.

But one group made very little noise about their support of Jimmy Carter—the born-again Christians. They remained quiet despite the fact that they probably gave Carter more votes than any other single category of people.

Jimmy Carter received almost the same percentage of the black vote in 1976 (93%) as George McGovern did in 1972 (92%).

And while I was not able to find any reliable figures as to how many millions of born-again Christians voted for Nixon or Wallace in 1968 and for Nixon in 1972, but switched to Carter in 1976, I think it's fair to say that between 5 million and 7.5 million switched.

So it's clear that the born-again Christians were much more important to Jimmy Carter than the blacks. And it's also clear that the blacks can be assumed to always vote for the Democratic candidate regardless of who the nominee is. Even George Wallace running against a racially moderate Republican for Governor of Alabama in 1974 received a majority of the black vote.

So the blacks have sent a message loud and clear to the politicians—they are Democrats and, regardless of the candidate, they will vote Democrat.

But the born-again Christians clearly are not married to any political party as are the blacks, union officials, environmentalists and Naderites.

In light of these facts, it's difficult to understand why for almost four years Carter has given the born-again Christians the back of his hand.

The blacks, the McGovern supporters, Ralph Nader and his followers, the environmentalists, have all let President Carter know almost daily that they supported him in 1976 and that they want their just rewards.

But the born-again Christians have asked for nothing but to be left alone.

And what has been Jimmy Carter's response to his biggest and most important single issue group of supporters?

Not only has the Carter administration ignored the born-again Christians, it has actively and aggressively sought to hurt the Christian movement in America.

For example, the IRS, whose head was appointed by Carter and can be removed by Carter, has made a major effort to put the Christian school movement out of business by saying that any private school started after 1953 is presumed to be "racist" until it meets affirmative action standards proposed by IRS. A "racist" school would lose its tax-deductible status, which means it would most likely have to shut its doors.

For example, Carter and his aides have indicated that if Congress passed a law that would allow voluntary prayer in public schools he would veto it.

For another example, Carter has not appointed to high government office a single clearly identified fundamentalist Christian. Instead, he is surrounded by many people who routinely reject Biblical principles regarding sexual behavior, family responsibility, abortion and other key moral issues.

It is hard to believe that Carter has been so callous to his most important and biggest supporters of 1976. But it's true.

He had a golden opportunity in July and August 1979 when he made wholesale changes in his cabinet to try and get back in the good graces of born-again Christians, moral majority Americans, fed-up taxpayers.

But Carter ignored these groups. Instead, he drew his appointments from the same old crowd of liberals and big businessmen—picking people like Patricia Harris, G. William Miller, Moon Landrieu and Neil Goldschmidt.

Two of the most basic rules of politics are that you must have a base of support and you must protect that base of support.

But Carter did not even know what his real base of support was. He obviously thought it was the union officials, the environmentalists, the McGovern liberals in the Democratic Party.

But as he learned in the primaries during the first half of 1980, a large chunk of that liberal-labor coalition backed Teddy Kennedy. And now much of the liberal establishment is off raising money and getting votes for John Anderson.

Carter is also wrapping the American flag around him with his failed attempt to rescue the American hostages in Iran, his tough talk regarding the Soviets and his call for more defense spending. It's probable that Carter survived Kennedy and even kept a neo-conservative out of the Democratic race with his "tough" patriotic talk in the last part of 1979 and first half of 1980.

But all these unhappy groups in America—the taxpayer, the born-again Christian, the pro-defense citizen, the moral majority American—are actively looking for an alternative to Jimmy Carter.

Government assaults on church rights aren't all that are bothering conservative Christians.

So are government attacks on the family, like the Supreme Court's original 1973 pro-abortion decision, the Equal Rights Amendment, plans to draft women, and various homosexual rights ordinances.

As a result, conservative Christians—particularly fundamentalist Protestants—are getting politically concerned.

Evangelists like Jerry Falwell, James Robison, and Pat Robertson, who reach over 20 million people by television every week, are talking about political issues and urging their listeners to register to vote and get involved in politics.

Separation of church and state, they remind their audiences, does not mean separation of God and government.

"The only hope for America," says Rev. Falwell, "is to awaken the religious people of America." He adds that preachers must get involved in politics since the "leadership of godly men is the best available."

Rev. Falwell practices what he preaches. He has probably done more than any other person to block passage of ERA in Virginia.

Reflecting the deep patriotism of most evangelists, Rev. Falwell organized in July 1979 a 12,000-person pro-American rally on the steps of the U.S. Capitol. Among the New Right leaders who addressed the rally were Sen. Jesse Helms, Sen. Gordon Humphrey, Congressman Robert Dornan and others.

Pat Robertson, who started the Christian Broadcasting Network (CBN) in 1960, which today reaches millions of TV viewers, urges Christians to get into the political arena so we can "place this nation under God."

"We have together," says Robertson, "with the Protestants and the Catholics, enough votes to run the country. And when the people say, 'We've had enough,' we are going to take over."

The Dallas Freedom Rally of Rev. James Robison in June 1979 showed that Christian people are ready. More than 12,000 people attended to protest against WFAA-TV Dallas, which threw evangelist Robison off the air in March because he preached against homosexuality.

The station claimed that Dr. Robison's sermon violated the Federal Communications Commission's Fairness Doctrine. A galaxy of religious and political stars spoke at the rally, including New Right leaders Howard Phillips and Paul Weyrich, who urged Christians to get more involved in politics.

Rev. Charles Stanley, pastor of the First Baptist Church of Atlanta, has reached over 1 million Americans with a videotape of his brilliant sermon, "Stand Up America," which calls on Christians to become active in politics.

Beyond question, Christians have already made their political presence felt.

• The IRS has abandoned, at least for the time being, its anti-church school campaign, primarily because Dr. Bob Billings, a New Right leader, organized a campaign that caused about 200,000 letters to be received by the IRS protesting their plans. At least another 200,000 letters and cards of protest were received by Jimmy Carter in the White House and Members of Congress.

• Rev. Robison's Freedom Rally raised $100,000 for legal expenses which were used successfully to force WFAA to put James Robison back on the air.

• Several states have passed laws protecting the independence of church schools.

In Indiana, it was the Church Freedom Legislative Package. The man behind the legislation was Greg Dixon, pastor of the 7,000 member Indianapolis Baptist Temple. His inspired preaching forced Marion County (Indianapolis) prosecutor James Kelley, who had made the city a haven for homosexuals, to announce he would not seek reelection.

Virginia recently passed a law denying the state jurisdiction over Christian day care centers. The North Carolina legislature has limited the state's authority over church schools to health and safety, leaving classes and teacher credentials in the hands of the schools.

I believe these victories will multiply as Bible-believing Americans get better and better organized. And they are.

Jerry Falwell, for example, has formed the Moral Majority, Inc., an organization that aims to mobilize millions of Americans to work for pro-God, pro-family policies in government.

From the end of November 1979 through July 1980, the Moral Majority and other Christian organizations registered 2.5 million new voters. Their goal by Election Day 1980 is to register a total of 5 million new Christian voters.

The Moral Majority has two arms—one for lobbying, one for education. The Moral Majority's executive director is Dr. Bob Billings, who has lobbied for years for Christian causes in the nation's capitol.

The Moral Majority won't directly help candidates, but it will give politically concerned Christians a way to meet and work with each other.

And conservative Christians can be very effective in a political campaign.

When New Right leader Donald E. (Buz) Lukens was first elected to Congress from Ohio in 1966, he had strong support from fundamentalist Christians. They made excellent workers because, as Lukens explains, they took their campaign commitment as a solemn personal responsibility. Buz also recalls that the endorsements he received from fundamentalist pastors were as stirring as any he has ever heard.

The foundation of the Moral Majority will be fundamentalist Protestants, in particular the estimated 15 million Americans who watch Falwell's "Old Time Gospel Hour" regularly. Rev. Falwell has a remarkable base to work with. He already has 2 million names on his "Gospel Hour" mailing list.

But Dr. Falwell intends to build a coalition of not only his own religious followers but of Catholics, Jews and Mormons. Significantly, New Right leaders Paul Weyrich, an Eastern Rite Catholic, and Howard Phillips, a Jew, worked closely with Falwell in setting up the Moral Majority.

The potential of such a coalition is tremendous. There are an estimated 85 million Americans—50 million born-again Protestants, 30 million morally conservative Catholics, 3 million Mormons and 2 million Orthodox and Conservative Jews—with whom to build a pro-family, Bible-believing coalition.

Church leaders acknowledge that overcoming age-old suspicions among Catholics, Protestants and Jews won't be easy. But increasing threats from big government and big business (like mass media fascination with exploiting sex) make coming together an absolute necessity.

Another new political group is Christian Voice, whose board includes New Right Senators Orrin Hatch, James McClure and Roger Jepsen. The Los Angeles-based organization enlisted 37,000 clergymen from 45 denominations by mid-1980. It has more than 187,000 members and an annual budget of $3 million.

Christian Voice plans to distribute TV and radio tapes with messages by Senators Helms and Hatch and Congressman Marvin Leath of Texas.

The group was active in both the Rhodesia and Taiwan fights. Its expected opposition to liberalized homosexual rights prompted Gay Rights National Lobby representative Steve Endean to admit: "This is probably the most significant threat to gay progress on issues before the Congress that we've faced."

Rev. Robert Grant, the chairman of Christian Voice, was one of the founders of American Christian Cause, which worked in Anita Bryant's Florida campaign and the California Briggs amendment efforts to limit homosexual influence.

In late September 1979, another major new conservative Christian organization was launched—The Religious Roundtable.

Founded by Ed McAteer, a businessman and lifelong Christian lay leader, Religious Roundtable meets four times a year for two days. Each two-day meeting will bring together 150 or more major Christian leaders. They will discuss which national, political and governmental issues they should alert their millions of followers to take action on when they return home.

I can think of no better example to describe the New Right. It is talented, aggressive leaders

163

meeting and deciding on a course of action in an important area. The Religious Roundtable is just one example of the type of coordinated, structured, conservative activity in a New Right area that didn't happen six years ago.

Through such leaders, the Roundtable aims to reach and activate tens of millions of other religious conservatives who may play a part when Congress considers legislation affecting abortion, private schools, prayer in schools, sex in the media and a strong national defense.

The first two-day session of the Religious Roundtable in September 1979 included remarks by Senator Gordon Humphrey, Phyllis Schlafly and New Right leaders Howard Phillips, Paul Weyrich, Richard Dingman of the House Study Committee and myself on practical politics. Also speaking were Houston pollster Lance Tarrance on the political opinions of Americans of various religious denominations and Clay Claiborne, director of the Black Silent Majority.

Some of the other religious leaders who attended the first meeting of the Religious Roundtable were:

• Dr. Bob Billings, executive director of Jerry Falwell's The Moral Majority.

• Dr. G. Cameron Townsend, founder of the Wycliffe Bible translators, with more than 15,000 missionaries in some 150 countries.

• Dr. Adrian Rogers, then president of the Southern Baptist Convention (1979-80), which represents 38,000 churches and 13 million Southern Baptists.

• Bob Dugan, director of public affairs for the National Association of Evangelicals, representing 35,000 churches of various denominations.

• John Talcott, founder and president of the Plymouth Rock Foundation, which prepares material for church school programs.

• Dr. Ben Armstrong, executive director of National Religious Broadcasting, representing 810 radio stations.

• John D. Beckett, president of Intercessors for America, a nationwide prayer organization.

• Bobby Richardson, former New York Yankees All-Star second baseman and popular banquet speaker for Christian causes.

There are many more Christian groups active across the country which can and should be mentioned.

The Cleveland law firm of Gibbs and Craze devotes five full-time lawyers to protecting Christian schools, foster homes and day care centers from bureaucratic assaults.

Pro-life groups of course depend heavily upon Catholics and conservative Protestants.

But there are others. Anita Bryant's campaign drew most of its members from Bible-believing Christians and Jews.

Mike Thompson, of Miami, Florida, who was communications director for the Bryant campaign, says flatly, "We put a new majority together in Dade County. We had the involvement of a total cross section of the community: Democrats, Republicans, Independents, all with the denominator of social conservatism."

Phyllis Schlafly's Stop-ERA and Eagle Forum have received strong support among church groups. When Schlafly and her allies organized the 1977 pro-family rally in Houston to counter

Bella Abzug's women's lib conference, Christian churches across America bused in many of the 20,000 people who attended.

Mormons are prominent in two newer pro-family groups—Pro-Family United, an educational organization, and United Families of America, a lobbying group. The Mormon Church, by opposing ERA and abortion, has encouraged countless Mormons to get involved in these two battles. Phyllis Schlafly readily admits that Mormons gave her Stop-ERA forces the margin of victory in Florida, Nevada and Virginia.

Across the country, conservative preachers are beginning to lead and speak out on politics just as liberals like Protestants Rev. Andrew Young, Rev. William Sloane Coffin, Rev. Martin Luther King, Jr. and Catholics Rev. Theodore Hesburgh and Father Robert Drinan did in the past.

During the 25 years that I've been active in politics, the major religious leaders in America have been liberals who were in the forefront of almost every political cause—civil rights battles, Vietnam war rallies, reduction in military spending, and expansion of welfare.

For example, the ultra-liberal National Council of Churches:

• Advocated the admission of Red China to the United Nations as early as 1958.

• Came out against prayer in the public schools in 1963.

• Spoke out against the war in Vietnam in 1965.

• Pushed for a guaranteed annual income.

• Pressed for more foreign aid year after year.

Liberals are now complaining about conservative ministers who are just doing what liberal ministers have been doing for decades.

Conservative ministers have just been unable to sit back and accept the ultra-liberal actions of the World Council of Churches and projects like its so-called Programme to Combat Racism.

The World Council shocked Christians around the World in August 1978 when it donated $85,000 to the pro-Marxist Patriotic Front of Zimbabwe (Rhodesia). The grant came shortly after the Patriotic Front boasted that it had shot down an unarmed Air Rhodesia airliner carrying civilians. The Front then denied it had any part in the massacre of the passengers who survived the crash.

According to the *New Republic*, the donation to the Patriotic Front ignited "a firestorm of protest" from Protestant clergy and laymen, revealing the gulf between the World Council and its constituency.

Christian Century, a liberal ecumenist magazine, described those who made the grant as "armchair guerrillas, vicarious doers of violence."

The Presbyterian Lay Committee, composed of members of United Presbyterian churches, accused the WCC of "subsidizing murderers" and urged the church to sever its ties with the world organization.

Catholics have been aroused by the continuing smear attacks on them because of their pro-life, anti-abortion stance. For example, Eleanor Smeal, president of the National Organization of Women (NOW), sent out a 1977 fund-raising letter which linked American

Nazis, John Birch Society members, Ku Klux Klanners, and Roman Catholic bishops.

Smeal charged: "The intimidation of state and national legislators by the Roman Catholic hierarchy is an exercise of political power that threatens the rights of all Americans."

That is not only nonsense, it is libelous. The Catholic bishops do take positions on matters like abortion—but speaking out firmly is not intimidation.

Conservative Christians are also taking to the political barricades because of pornography— not just at the newsstands and TV and movies but in the public schools.

You may remember the textbook controversy in Kanawha County, West Virginia, in 1975. Liberals tried to picture the protestors as a bunch of ignorant rednecks out to burn books. But what upset Mrs. Alice Moore and other conservative parents were passages like the following from *Blue Denim*, a play to be read aloud by 12-and 13-year olds:

"Ernie: At first he thought he'd get four other guys to swear she'd put out to *them* too, but then he decided he'd better do the honorable thing and get her an abortion."

And then there is television, the mass medium whose primary yardstick is, Does it sell? Apparently, sex sells very well.

Rev. Don Wildmon, founder of the National Federation for Decency, has reported:

• In the fall of the 1977, 1978 and 1979 seasons, almost 90% of all sex on TV was outside of marriage.

• During an average year of prime-time viewing, the TV audience is exposed to 11,531 sexually suggestive comments or scenes of implied sexual intercourse. If "skin scenes" (undue and unnecessary emphasis on the female anatomy) are added, the total rises to 18,429.

• During the 1979 monitoring period, the amount of profanity on the networks increased by 45.47% over a comparable 1978 period. A clear trend toward "hard profanity" is evident.

Don't say there's nothing you can do about it.

Rev. Don Wildmon has led several successful boycotts against advertisers on immoral programs.

In 1979, Rev. Wildmon headed a national boycott of Kentucky Fried Chicken because the company's owner, Heublein Corp., was sponsoring so much pornography on TV. As a result, Kentucky Fried Chicken is now limiting its advertising to news and children's programs.

The year before, he led a nationwide demonstration in 32 cities against Sears and Roebuck for its sponsorship of unwholesome TV programs. You know what? On the day of the demonstration, Sears withdrew its advertising from two of TV's most sexually provocative programs—"Three's Company" and "Charlie's Angels."

The trend toward so-called "soft pornography" on TV must and can be stopped. If we don't act, the "porn" will get a little harder and a little more explicit each year.

That's what has happened with movies, books and magazines. A certain level of pornography is reached, and at first a majority of Americans are shocked and offended.

But after a while, people begin to feel they can't do anything about it. They accept what they see and hear. And the pornographers then reach for the next level.

That's the way the magazines went. First, there was *Esquire*, which in comparison with other "men's magazines" today seems as tame as *Jack and Jill*. Then came *Playboy*. Then *Penthouse*, then *Hustler* and a whole group of hardcore pornographic magazines which make a mockery of free speech.

Can this trend be stopped? Of course it can. And it can be done without violating the U.S. Constitution. The First Amendment was not designed to protect pornographers.

In the final analysis, it's up to each and every one of us.

Each American shares the responsibility to make America great again. We must use whatever talents God has given us.

This can take many directions. Community work, church activity and political involvement are just a few.

However, there are two things all of us can and should do which are more important than any other actions we could undertake. These are prayer and fasting.

I wrote in *Conservative Digest* in May/June, 1980 about the need for Americans to fast and ask God for forgiveness of our sins, ask for His protection, and give thanks for His blessings.

I proposed a National Day of Prayer and Fasting.

I urged Americans to petition Congress to proclaim the Sunday before Thanksgiving as a National Day of Prayer and Fasting.

I suggested this particular day because this is traditionally a time when Americans give thanks to God for all the blessings that we enjoy.

It would be a true and appropriate commemoration of the Thanksgiving season. And I feel it would make the spirit of Thanksgiving more meaningful to us.

George Washington set aside a day of fasting and prayer when he was President.

Also Abraham Lincoln, twice during the storm of our tragic Civil War, designated "a Sunday for prayer and fasting."

Twice during some of the darkest days of the American Revolutionary War, the Continental Congress declared a day of Fasting and Repentance.

Indeed, even Christ, when He knew He was soon to be tempted by the devil, prayed and fasted for 40 days.

The Bible tells us that bread cast upon water will return. And that you reap what you sow. I believe this is true for nations as well as individuals.

America was founded upon a belief in God. Our motto, "In God We Trust," reflects that belief. And as long as America held fast to that belief, God blessed us.

About 15 years ago, America's problems seemed to significantly increase.

Civil unrest, racial strife, a lost war in Vietnam, illegal drug use, soaring inflation, a declining business climate, attacks on the family, sex and pornography in the movies and on TV, a lack of presidential leadership, a weak U.S. military and a strong and aggressive Soviet military are some examples of our major problems.

Today, world and national events look grim.

But as we look to the future, we shouldn't do so with worry and pessimism.

We worry when we see the Communists gaining military strength daily, and when our President seems uninterested in opposing the Communist conquest of country after country.

But instead of worrying, why don't we as individuals and as a nation go to God and ask forgiveness for our sins?

Instead of worrying, why don't we pray that He protect America from its enemies and give us the strength and will to protect ourselves?

Why don't we thank God for the benefits He has bestowed on us as individuals and as a nation?

Perhaps many of our personal and national problems have developed because we have forgotten to thank God for our blessings, our opportunities, our freedoms and our great country.

The power of millions of Americans praying together for a common goal can have a profound effect.

That's why I'm asking you to help establish a National Day of Prayer and Fasting.

This day will symbolize America's desire to return to God. It will focus our attention on the reasons why God blessed us and challenges us today.

Almost everyone I have discussed the National Day of Prayer and Fasting with is enthusiastic.

One minister, Reverend Claude Pike, told me that after reading my article, he decided to devote most of his time flying a 50-year-old Bellanca Pacemaker airplane with his sons across

America to help promote a National Day of Prayer and Fasting.

Vermont Governor Richard Snelling issued an official proclamation setting aside November 18, 1979, as a day of prayer, fasting and recollection.

Many people have told me they will help, but your help is needed to make a National Day of Prayer and Fasting become an annual observance.

Please sign the petition in the Appendix. Ask others to sign it too.

Then make photocopies and mail the copies to every local, state and national government official you can think of, including the President, congressmen, senators, governors, mayors, state legislators and city councilmen.

Write to the editors of newspapers and magazines and call in to radio and TV talk shows.

Ask the religious, business, fraternal and social groups to which you belong to adopt this statement as an official proclamation. Then mail the proclamation to your elected public officials.

I hope we can encourage enough people to join with us to persuade the President and Congress and every governor and every mayor and every county executive to make the National Day of Prayer and Fasting an annual observance on the Sunday before Thanksgiving right across the country.

With your help and your prayers, it will become a reality.

By the way, I believe that those who want to play a leadership role in saving America and bringing freedom to the world should set aside not just one day a year, but one or more days a month exclusively devoted to prayer, fasting and meditation.

I believe that if we do, miracles will come to pass in our lives and in our country.

Remember, we are trying to take power away from those who govern this country and the world. And they are not going to give it up without a very, very tough, hard fight.

And we're not going to succeed without God's help.

Please include the men and women who are leading the fight for freedom in this country in your daily prayers.

IX

The Tax Revolt

For about 150 years in our history, until the late 1920's, total government spending stayed almost the same—about 10% of national income. And income taxes remained quite low—from a minimum of about 1% to a maximum of 24% in 1925.

However, since the election of Franklin D. Roosevelt in 1932 and the liberal takeover of the nation's capital, government spending and government taxes have exploded.

So much so that today, Americans appear ready to fight to the death against taxes and spending in a national rebellion from California to Washington, D.C.

According to Nobel economist Milton Friedman, "Total government spending — state, federal and local — (now) amounts to 40% of the national income."

In 1979, reports Don Lambro in his definitive book, *Fat City*, a typical taxpayer with a wife and two children earning $18,000 a year paid an "astounding $4,814 in federal taxes, including income, social security, excise and other levies."

The lion's share of personal income taxes, journalists Sheldon Engelmayer and Robert Wagman report, is paid by people having incomes between $17,000 and $40,000. Once your income goes over $17,000, you are in the top 50% of earners in America, and the top 50% pays 92% of all taxes, according to the IRS.

It took the federal government 175 years for its annual budget to reach $100 billion. It then took only nine years, from 1962 to 1971, for the federal budget to pass the $200 billion mark. It took another four years to hit $300 billion and just another two years to go over $400 billion.

By 1979, the federal government was spending almost $500 billion a year and reaching for $550 billion. The 1981 budget is expected to top $616 billion — easily.

At the same time, the government has consistently been spending more than it has taken in — running up deficits in 25 of the last 30 years. And it has had to borrow heavily to make up the difference. The 1980 deficit is expected to top $60 billion, with the government's total debt to reach (are you ready?) $859.2 billion.

Federal budget planners, says Lambro, have predicted that the total federal debt will be $951.9 billion by 1982 — almost $1 trillion. The interest payments alone will be about $57 billion in 1980.

This kind of irresponsible deficit spending by liberals has produced double-digit inflation, crushing taxes, soaring unemployment, and an aroused American public.

176

As Howard Jarvis might put it, "We're mad as hell and we're not going to take this anymore!"

The overwhelming passage of Proposition 13 in California in 1978, severely limiting property taxes, was felt across the country.

• Jeff Bell, a 34-year-old economist who never ran before for public office, beat New Jersey's four-term U.S. Senator, liberal Clifford Case, in the GOP primary that year. Bell's main campaign theme: a call for a one-third cut in personal income taxes.

• In the spring of 1978, Tennessee voted to limit tax increases to the rate of growth of the state's economy — the first state ever to adopt a constitutional spending limitation.

• Since then, Hawaii, Texas, Michigan, Arizona, Washington and California have all placed various legal lids on their states' spending. Colorado is the only state where voters rejected a constitutional spending limit — in 1978.

• Congressman Jack Kemp of New York and Senator William Roth of Delaware introduced their now-famous Kemp-Roth bill to cut federal income taxes one-third over a period of three years.

Tax cuts are not only good politics but good economics, too.

UCLA economist Arthur Laffer, a top advisor to Congressman Kemp, argues that taxes in America are so high they discourage companies from expanding and employees from trying to make more money. Laffer says that a tax cut would unleash new economic energies which would greatly expand the tax base. The result: the government would lose little in total tax receipts or actually take in more as lower tax rates generated more taxable income for all Americans.

Neo-conservative columnist Michael Novak puts it this way:

"For the first time in 40 years, the Republicans are in a position to offer more than Democrats: 'More of your own money in your own pocket.'

" 'Keep it out of the hands of government,' the Republicans can now say. 'Keep more of it for yourself.' "

If we do not act, and soon, the United States could go the way of Great Britain.

Already, many of our factories and machines have become outmoded. Our industrial cities have run down. Our work force has become less productive.

Real growth has declined in the face of high taxes and crushing government regulation. In short, as *Time* magazine has commented, America "is losing its economic edge in the world, and the hour is late — very late."

Frankly, what we must do is stop socialism.

Thirty-two years ago, liberal philosopher Arthur Schlesinger, Jr., wrote in *Partisan Review* that he saw "no inherent obstacle to the gradual advance of socialism in the United States through a series of New Deals."

He was right. Our marvelous system of government, though created by patriots of great genius, does not adequately protect private citizens against the power of big government.

Local, state and national legislators have proved unable to resist the demands for more money by bureaucrats and the thousands of pleas by liberal do-gooders (and socialists) who insist on doing "good" with someone else's money.

"It is the first principle of politics where (Teddy) Kennedy comes from," columnist Joseph Sobran wrote, "that when you *care* about people, you show it by spending other people's money on them."

Even candidates who win election honestly, intending to cut spending and taxes, often collapse when the highly effective liberals apply pressure.

And, of course, some candidates try to fool the voters by saying anything to get elected. Once elected, a politician has the advantage of incumbency and can often win reelection even if he breaks his promise to fight big spending. Besides that, with our combination of inflation and the progressive tax rate, members of Congress can have their expanded government programs and never have to vote for a tax increase.

Fifteen years ago, Morton Blackwell asked Milton Friedman if the growth of government could be stopped. Yes, he replied, but only if that growth becomes so rapid and painful that citizens will rise up and fight to turn back the trend while there is still enough strength left in the private sector to resist the invasion of government.

The citizen's revolt is here and now. The tax, spend and elect system begun by Franklin D. Roosevelt is bearing the bitter fruit of inflation, recession and unemployment.

Our economy is suffering from the worst period of inflation since Alexander Hamilton stabilized the dollar almost 200 years ago.

Our government, at all levels, eats up about half of each dollar our free enterprise system produces.

Businessmen are so over-regulated and harassed by bureaucrats that they are approaching the point of zero economic freedom.

In the auto industry, *Newsweek* reported in March 1979, government fuel efficiency and safety standards over the past decade have added as much as $600 to the price of every car. Those air bags being promoted so aggressively by Ralph Nader would add another $500 to every auto.

OSHA's initial proposal to limit noise in the workplace would cost an estimated $10 billion. EPA's original plan to maintain what it considers an "acceptable" ozone level in the atmosphere could have run as high as $20 billion. Pollution control in 1980, according to *Newsweek*, will cost state and local governments as well as industry over $14 billion.

The statewide campaigns I have mentioned as well as hundreds of local efforts attest to the continuing strength of the national tax rebellion.

But state and local antitax victories aren't enough. If every state and every local government limited their taxes and balanced their budget, that would not halt the gradual advance of socialism at the most important level — the federal government.

Congress has shown again and again that it cannot discipline itself. We must, as Thomas Jefferson said, "bind them down with the chains of the Constitution."

The relentless growth of our federal government can be stopped. We can do it by amending our Constitution and plugging up the loopholes by which the federal government is gradually destroying our economic freedom and thereby all our freedoms.

There are two exciting proposals which together form what this country needs so badly — a firm and unyielding obstacle to socialism that Arthur Schlesinger, Jr., accurately saw did not exist 32 years ago.

First is the balanced budget proposal which is being shepherded by the National Taxpayers Union, headed by James Davidson. As of this writing, 29 state legislatures have petitioned the Congress to call a constitutional convention for a balanced budget amendment to our Constitution. When five more states join these 29, Congress must either call the convention or pass a balanced budget Constitutional amendment.

The second proposal is the spending limitation amendment being sponsored by the National Tax Limitation Committee, directed by Lewis Uhler, a former top Reagan aide in California who authored the historic state tax-limitation amendment, Proposition 1, in 1973. The NTLC amendment, largely the brainchild of Dr. Friedman, was introduced in the Congress in April 1979 by Sen. Richard Stone of Florida, a Democrat, and Sen. H. J. Heinz III of Pennsylvania, a Republican.

This amendment would reverse the trend of increasing tax bites and stop the process by which government gets a bigger cut of your income as inflation pushes you into higher tax brackets.

Both these proposals contain safeguards to permit higher spending in times of real national emergency, such as war or other national calamity.

We conservatives must strike while the iron is hot. If we are ever going to put a halt to big government, we must not let this chance slip through our fingers. We must channel the fierce public uproar over inflation and high taxes into effective action now.

It's going to be a hard fight. Most of the bureaucrats, big labor, big media, and the liberals and socialists will fight us tooth and nail against these two amendments.

They will try to talk them to death. They will try to frighten voters just as California liberals tried to do prior to the passage of Proposition 13 in 1978. They failed then, but the liberals were successful in June 1980 in scaring the voters of California into voting against Proposition 9, which would have cut state income tax rates by half.

Our victories will not come easily. If there were an easy solution, we'd have stopped the growth of big government long ago. But this is a fight we *can* and must win for all Americans.

Both the balanced budget and the spending limitation amendments are good and needed. Together they will work an economic miracle in America.

We must make it as politically painful as possible for a U.S. Senator, Congressman or state legislator to oppose either amendment. Don't let any liberal wriggle off the hook by supporting only one of the amendments. America needs both.

Let your elected representatives know you're watching them like a hawk, waiting to see how hard they fight to pass these amendments. Don't let up on them until you win their active support for both.

And don't let your friends be fooled by liberal claims that these amendments are too restrictive, that the politicians need more "flexibility." Liberal flexibility has stopped our country's economic growth and produced a kind of rubber money that just won't stretch any more.

There is one other thing we must do and that is stop the waste in Washington. Don Lambro, one of UPI's finest investigative reporters, spent three years researching and writing *Fat City*, (Regnery/Gateway, Inc., 1980) which should be read by every taxpayer.

Lambro estimates that "at least $100 billion a year in taxes is unnecessarily going to the federal government to be squandered on programs our country could better do without."

Think of it — $100 billion a year, nearly one-sixth of the annual federal budget.

Here are just a few of the 100 federal programs proposed for the ax by Don Lambro as outlined by editor Marvin Stone of *U.S. News & World Report:*

• Community Services Administration, $668 million. The 800 local Community Action Programs supported in part by the CSA should exist with the consent of state and local elected officials rather than continue as costly, ineffective appendages of the federal bureaucracy.

• Youth Conservation Corps, $70 million. It aids mostly white, middle-class young people who are already employable and don't need government help.

• Government film-making, $500 million. Most of the films are "frivolous, self-promoting and duplicative." A few film titles will tell you all you need to know: "Your Teeth Are in Your Hands" (a $35,000 film series made by the Navy to instruct recruits on how to care for their teeth); "Mulligan Stew" (a $300,000 film of the Agriculture Department, to teach children about good nutrition, a subject already taught in every school system in America); "America on the Rocks" (a $375,000 film by HEW, which discovered that alcoholism is a middle-class problem).

The National Endowment for the Arts reached a new low by underwriting one-third of the cost of a 30-minute film showing a dog being shot to death again and again.

• The U.S. Travel Service, $8 million. It duplicates work done better by non-government organizations.

• The Small Business Administration, $1.5 billion. An agency, in the words of Marvin Stone, "full of mismanagement, political favoritism and outright fraud."

• The Alaska Railroad, $8 million. The government should sell the railroad to private enterprise or turn it over to the state of Alaska.

• Highway Beautification Program, $20.5 million. State control programs and local community sign laws are adequate enough to deal with any billboard problem.

• The Federal Election Commission, $8.5 million. The FEC, Lambro wrote, "has heaped bureaucratic supervision and harassment and censorship upon our most fundamental . . . right."

• Federal Trade Commission. $65 million. The FTC, says Lambro, "is a supremely unnecessary and wasteful federal agency that the nation can no longer afford."

• Council on Wage and Price Stability, $5.9 million. "The place to start cutting the federal budget," argues Lambro, "would be to abolish this agency."

Please note that none of the above or any of the programs listed in *Fat City* would seriously threaten services and benefits for the poor, the sick, the elderly, the disabled, the jobless.

Lambro declares, "Government can be significantly reduced in size, and not a single truly needy American has to be denied benefits and services he or she truly deserves."

In fact, the reductions proposed in *Fat City* would provide more for the disadvantaged just as Ronald Reagan's welfare reform in California resulted in increased benefits for those truly in need.

And of course the elimination of wasteful programs would mean a reduction in the taxes needed for such programs, enabling Americans to better care for themselves.

In addition to wasteful programs which ought to be eliminated, Don Lambro describes wasteful practices which our federal government ought to stop without delay. Here are some of the more flagrant examples:

• The government loses more than $500 million a year in bad debts—such as from small business loans or Veterans Administration over-payments—which are routinely written off as "uncollectible."

The Department of Education admitted in July 1980 that 875,000 former students have defaulted on government education loans totalling $731.7 million, a default rate of 16%.

• White-collar cheaters and swindlers are reaping an estimated $15 billion (according to the Government Accounting Office) from federal economic assistance programs.

• Nearly 4,000 audit reports "are gathering dust on government shelves," although they document the loss of $4.3 billion annually in unauthorized use of federal funds by contractors and grant recipients.

• Federal employees now spend nearly $8 billion a year on travel — much of it first class. In 1976, the Small Business Administration (4,300 employees) spent $4.7 million on travel — over $1,000 for every secretary, billing clerk and manager.

Thomas Sowell, a black economics professor at UCLA, has summed up federal poverty programs:

"To be blunt, the poor are a gold mine. By the time they are studied, advised, experimented with, and administered, the poor have helped many a middle-class liberal to achieve affluence with government money."

Writing in the *New York Times Magazine*, Sowell said, "The total amount of money the government spends on its many antipoverty efforts is three times what would be required to lift every man, woman and child in America above the official poverty line by simply sending money to the poor."

Yes, as always, it is the poor who suffer the most from inflation, from taxation, from regulation, from liberalism.

Inflation makes the poor poorer. Taxes push up prices. Laws like the minimum wage prevent the poor from getting jobs. And liberalism offers the poor a handout while placing its foot on their neck.

The wealthy do most of the complaining, as J. Kesner Kahn says, but have the wealth to avoid real suffering. The middle class loses the most. But the poor who already do not have enough for their needs suffer the most from inflation and taxes because they must get along on even less.

New Right leader Howard Phillips, chosen by Nixon in 1973 to undertake the dismantling of the Office of Economic Opportunity, recalls: "I visited health programs where the main concern was registering voters. ... 81% of OEO's funds went in one form or another to overhead costs."

• The federal government is spending more than $1.5 billion every year "to promote, communicate and sell" its programs and accomplishments to the American people. There is now an army of nearly 20,000 "public relations" specialists in the various federal departments and agencies. The $1.5 billion includes the previously mentioned $500 million for audio-visual programs, more than $200 million for advertising and about $400 million for all other PR and public information programs, including the salaries of that 20,000 person federal "army."

• The Department of Labor's job-training program (CETA) is riddled with waste and mismanagement. In Nashville, Tenn., $12,000 was spent in 1979 to teach adults to "groom properly and use the telephone effectively." CETA is financing a body-building course for Pittsburgh women who want to work in the steel mills.

• In 1978, the Labor Department gave Cesar Chavez $500,000 to teach English to members of his militant ultra-liberal United Farm Workers.

• American business annually spends $32 billion, reports Lambro, to comply with the paperwork demands of Washington. It costs individuals, that is, you and me, nearly $9 billion a year to meet their paperwork requirements, mostly tax forms. The federal government spends more than $43 billion to print, process, compile and store federal forms. Lambro estimates that at least $100 billion "is sucked from our economy to comply with this paperwork passion."

Here is the laughable response of one government agency as revealed by the House Republican Study Committee: The Environmental Protection Agency has reduced one of its forms to one page but you must read a 90 page introduction of instructions to fill it out.

Then there is OSHA — the Occupational Safety and Health Administration — "Washington's most hated agency," to use Lambro's phrase.

Since 1970, when it was created, OSHA has been responsible for overseeing 6 million American businesses having one or more employees. The result has not been an improvement in health and safety among American businesses but deepening anger, resentment and contempt of OSHA.

It's easy to understand why when you consider the sheer stupidity of many of OSHA's demands:

— An OSHA inspector told a Florida meatpacking company a safety railing had to be put around its loading dock to keep workers from falling off. After the company put up the railing, an Agriculture Department inspector ordered it removed as an obstacle to sanitation.

— A Massachusetts supermarket was ordered to install a nonslip grating on its workspace floor. Along came Agriculture again, and the market was forced to rip out the grating and install a sanitary tile floor. Cost to the store (and ultimately to the store's customers): $25,000.

— The University of Illinois was forced to spend $557,000 when OSHA ruled that railings along an elevated walkway connecting campus buildings were a few inches too short. OSHA required all such railings be exactly 42 inches high.

Some American businessmen have fought back, most notably Ferrol G. (Bill) Barlow of Pocatello, Idaho.

In September 1975, an OSHA inspector, unexpected and unannounced, walked into Barlow's small heating and plumbing shop. Barlow politely refused him admission, citing the Fourth Amendment as protecting him "against unreasonable searches." Barlow said he would be happy to comply *if* the OSHA agent could produce a search warrant that provided a probable cause for OSHA to believe that some violation existed in the Barlow shop.

A legal battle followed, all the way to the U.S. District Court in Idaho, where a three-judge panel ruled in Barlow's favor, and finally to the U.S. Supreme Court, which agreed that OSHA must produce a search warrant if the employer demands it. It was a satisfying but expensive victory, with legal costs for Barlow of more than $100,000.

• The National Science Foundation has a passion for spending taxpayers' money on sex-related research projects. They have included a $121,000 grant to determine the effect of marijuana on men's ability to become sexually aroused. The NSF has also given away $40,000 on a study of the origins of Polynesian culture, $200,000 on the speech patterns of the people of Philadelphia, $22,000 on polygamy among birds, $24,000 on the reproductive strategies of milkweeds, and $81,300 on the sociosexual behavior of the dabbing African black duck.

• Since the Department of Housing and Urban Development (HUD) was established in 1965, it has spent more than $76 billion to provide decent housing for Americans. The result, in Lambro's words, "has been an enormous $76 billion disappointment." Millions of Americans still live in substandard urban and rural housing.

According to the government, federal housing programs have financed the construction of more than 1 million housing units. Yet with HUD's $76 billion, Lambro points out, the government "could have bought — at today's inflated prices — more than 1.5 million new $50,000 single-family homes."

What went wrong was summed up by *Washington Post* reporter Jackson Diehl in a 1979 article, entitled "Ghostly Remains":

"Billions of tax dollars were spent nationally — and millions were poured into the Pumpkin Hill apartments (in South Laurel, Maryland) — in pursuit of this Kennedy-Johnson dream of decent, affordable housing for every American.

"What millions of tax dollars bought in the case of Pumpkin Hill are apartments that Prince George's County Executive Lawrence J. Hogan recently called, 'threats to human life.'

"Pumpkin Hill, moreover, is one of six federally subsidized housing fiascoes in Prince George's County. Almost $35 million — five times the amount the government set out to spend — has been poured into the Pumpkin Hill, Central Gardens, Washington Heights, Baber Village, Nalley and Glenarden apartment projects.

"What HUD has to show for that $35 million today are six ugly and dangerous suburban slums.

"The big losers — besides the taxpayers — are the very people that the 2,140 apartment units were built to help."

Diehl's story, according to Lambro, "has been written in most major cities in the country." The greatest tragedy of all, he adds, is that:

"Instead of the poor, it is the banks, private developers, investors, consultants, contractors, and their own employees who have been among HUD's most successful beneficiaries."

The same could be said of federal program after federal program.

I could go on and on giving you more and more horror stories, but I'm sure the point of how Washington wastes our taxes had been made.

I now think, and hope, that I'm going to shock you by saying, you and I are basically responsible for Fat City. And it is up to you and to me to change it.

You and I have allowed politicians and bureaucrats to use *our* government and *our* tax dollars for their special greedy ends. But we can stop them if we choose to. How? I've already suggested a few ways in this chapter. Let me repeat them and add a few more possibilities.

1. *Support the federal balanced budget amendment* of the National Taxpayers Union.

2. *Back the spending limitation amendment* of the National Tax Limitation Committee.

3. *Work in your state for* the passage of *a balanced budget amendment* if you don't already have one.

4. Support legislation or a constitutional amendment that would *require 4% of the federal budget to be set aside* each year *for the repayment of the Federal debt.*

5. *Support* legislation or a constitutional amendment that would place *a limit on the federal income tax rate.* As Congressman Phil Crane has said, referring to the religious custom of tithing: "If God asks for 10%, Caesar should ask for no more."

Milton Friedman has estimated that an across the board tax rate of less than 20%, without any tax deductions except for strict job expenses, would produce more federal revenue than the present system.

6. *Do away with the monopoly the U.S. Post Office* now has on the delivery of the mail.

7. *Limit federal pay.* Most government employees collect more salary and more fringe benefits than private workers in comparable jobs. A federal job is a privilege, not a right.

8. *Limit government pensions.* Former Budget Director Charles Zwick reported in April 1978 that military pensions alone will hit $30 billion a year in 20 years. A typical federal civil service

worker, retiring at 55 after 30 years, would get $465,000 in benefits in a normal life span. A typical retiree from the private sector at age 62 can anticipate a pension of only $135,000.

9. Social security was never intended to be the sole support of our senior citizens. Sensible reform is long overdue, including abolition of the provision which prohibits people from earning more than $3,720 a year before age 65 and $5,000 a year over age 65 and still receiving their full benefits. What business is it of the government how much they make? They've paid into the system all of their lives, and they are entitled to their monthly check.

10. *Do away with all the unreasonable and unnecessary regulations* of OSHA, EPA, EEOC, CPSC, and every other alphabet agency in Washington.

One of many consumer-protection laws that completely backfired involved children's sleepwear. As reported by Marjorie Boyd in the September 1977 issue of the *Washington Monthly*, the Consumer Product Safety Commission in 1972 required that all children's sleepwear under size 6X be treated with a flame-retardant chemical. Millions of parents watched prices jump by 20% overnight.

Then five years later, the CPSC banned Tris, which had been used to treat over 40% of children's sleepwear. The reason: Tris had been discovered to be a cancer-causing agent.

The average fast-food hamburger is subject to 41,000 federal and state regulations, says *U.S. News & World Report.*

11. *Reduce the minimum wage*, starting with a differential for young people. As economist Dr. Walter Williams of Temple University and

other economists have shown, a higher and higher minimum wage drives up the cost of living and prevents employers from hiring the young and inexperienced jobseeker.

12. *Stop government handouts to liberal organizations. Conservative Digest* reported in its October 1979 issue that Americans for Democratic Action, the Sierra Club, the Environmental Defense Fund, the Naderite Center for Automobile Safety and other liberal groups "are increasingly being financed" by the Federal government. ADA's Washington chapter alone got $78,505.50 in 1978-79 to help private citizens testify at regulatory agency hearings. You know which part of the philosophical spectrum the ADA's "private citizens" came from.

13. *Support the "workfare" experiment* proposed by Congressman Paul Findley of Illinois, which would require welfare recipients to work off their benefits at the minimum wage. Food-stamp experiments have showed that two-thirds of the beneficiaries dropped out of the program or failed to show up when forced to work off their food stamps.

14. *Cut federal and state taxes significantly* so that the American system can be allowed to do what it does best — provide the maximum amount of prosperity for the greatest number of people.

X

The Pro-Family Movement and the New Right

Today, many liberals are declaring that the traditional family is dead. Well, there are lots of available statistics that suggest that while not dead, the American family is far from healthy.

• Nearly 1 out of every 2 marriages now ends in divorce.

• Nationally, one out of every five births is illegitimate. In 1978, there were more illegitimate than legitimate births in both New York City and Washington, D.C.

• There were an estimated 12 million cases of venereal disease among young people in 1979, according to the U.S. Surgeon General.

• There have been an estimated 1 million abortions a year in America since the Supreme Court decision of January 1973.

• Six out of 10 married women with school-age children work.

• In Los Angeles alone, 30,000 children are being exploited for pornographic books, magazines, films and prostitution.

195

At the 1978 convention of the National Right to Life Committee, Dr. Harold Voth, a senior psychiatrist at the Menninger Foundation, declared that the fundamental unit of every society is the family which, in his professional opinion, is deteriorating in modern America.

American pioneers were strong, God-fearing and family-oriented. They built houses and families to last. They lived, worked and died together.

But, said Dr. Voth, industrialization, wars, economic pressures and working mothers have all combined to deprive children of good parenting. And without good committed parents, there can be few healthy children. And without healthy children, a society soon loses its vitality.

There is an urgent need, the Menninger psychiatrist argued, to make the family flourish again, to fight anti-family organizations like the National Organization of Women and to resist laws like the Equal Rights Amendment that attack families and individuals.

"Strong families and strong leaders built this country," said Dr. Voth, "and strong families and strong leaders will save it."

Which is what the pro-family movement aims to do. Paul Weyrich, a leader of the New Right and of this new pro-family coalition, believes that family issues in the 1980's could be what Vietnam was in the 1960's and environmental and consumer issues were in the 1970's for the left.

Millions of Americans have been politically awakened by such issues as:

• May our children pray at school?

- Should children be flooded with pornography?
- Should wives and mothers be drafted into our armed forces?
- Should abortions be encouraged by the federal government?
- Should the federal government regulate relations between husband and wife, between parent and child?

The pro-family movement is an incredibly dynamic coalition of groups — many of which didn't exist a year ago. And most of whose members are getting into politics for the first time.

The pro-family movement has enormous political strength — in its outreach and in its moral commitment. As Paul Weyrich says, "As pro-family groups become better educated in the political process, a lot of Congressmen who today thumb their noses at the whole notion of a pro-family coalition are going to be humbled."

Because so many anti-family laws and regulations flow from Washington, D.C., pro-family leaders set up an organization in the nation's capital in the summer of 1979. They call themselves "Library Court," after the tiny street on Capitol Hill where the original meeting place was located. The coalition represents more than 20 national groups.

They have gotten off to a fast start. In 1979, the Library Court group sponsored a flood of letters to the Department of Health, Education and Welfare protesting its plans for test-tube baby research. Their campaign forced HEW to put the project on the back burner.

In 1980, the group has fought both the Domestic Violence Bill — an unwarranted federal intrusion into family matters — and Sen. Edward Kennedy's Criminal Code Recodification Bill, which would enact ERA through the back door, weaken federal controls over pornography and legitimize homosexuality.

They are already a political force to be reckoned with.

Dr. William Gribbin, social policy analyst for the Senate Republican Policy Committee, says: "The organized pro-family effort, as manifested by Library Court meetings, has already made a major impact on the legislative process during the 96th Congress, and that impact is likely to grow in the future."

Members of Library Court are quick to emphasize that their first commitment is to traditional pro-family, pro-God values. They are political conservatives second, and sometimes not at all.

Jim Wright, chairman of the Maryland-based Christian Coalition for Legislative Action and one of Library Court's most active members, says that "the pro-family movement is not a subset of the conservative movement."

The pro-family movement is made up of people of all faiths — Catholic, Protestant, Jewish, Eastern Orthodox.

Paul Weyrich is very optimistic about the future impact of the pro-family movement. "In sheer numbers," he asserts, "the potential outreach of the Library Court group is greater than the whole range of conservative groups."

The chairman of Library Court is Mrs. Connaught (Connie) Marshner, director of the Family Policy Division of the Free Congress Foundation, and a tireless writer, speaker and debater. For example, in the first half of 1980, she spoke in a dozen states, appeared on such national talk shows as *The 700 Club*, and conducted an average of six interviews a week with major newspapers and magazines. Connie's book, *Blackboard Tyranny*, has become gospel for the education groups in the pro-family movement.

Some other members of Library Court include: Bob Baldwin, executive director, Citizens for Educational Freedom; Dr. Bob Billings, executive director, Moral Majority; Judie Brown, president, American Life Lobby; William Chasey, executive vice president for governmental and political affairs, the Religious Roundtable; Jack Clayton, Washington representative, American Association of Christian Schools; Sharon Pelton, social issues director, Conservatives Against Liberal Legislation; Susan Phillips, director of research and publications, The Conservative Caucus Research, Analysis and Education Foundation; Louise Ropog, administrative assistant, Family America; Kathy Teague, executive director, American Legislative Exchange Council, and Jim Wright, chairman, Christian Coalition for Legislative Action.

While the pro-family movement, like many New Right efforts, spends much of its time fighting liberal measures, it is also leading the campaign for a major new piece of legislation which would make wholesome family life a national priority.

The legislation is the Family Protection Act, introduced by Sen. Paul Laxalt of Nevada in September 1979. The Family Protection Act is a major project of the conservative movement.

Connie Marshner worked closely with Senator Laxalt in drafting the bill.

The act will be a benchmark for years to come for the kind of sensible actions the federal government should be taking to preserve traditional family values in America.

It reasserts the rights of parents in rearing and educating their children. It seeks to protect the rights of private schools. It gives parents a greater role in textbook review. It denies government favoritism for homosexuality.

In short, the bill attempts to reestablish the family as the basic unit of strength for America.

After introducing the Family Protection Act, Senator Laxalt hosted a luncheon for a group of the nation's top evangelical leaders who promised an all-out effort to pass the bill. Senator Laxalt said that "for years we have been debating on the terms of those who want to remake society. Now those groups will have to explain why they oppose the traditional idea of the family."

The legislation contains several unique tax ideas such as: a tax incentive for Americans to provide same-home care for their own parents; IRA (Individual Retirement Account) -type savings accounts which would enable parents to save money for the education of their children; IRA's for spouses; and repeal of the inequities of the marriage tax.

The Family Protection Act is a detailed piece of legislation running over 50 pages. Here are some of the major sections contained in the Act:

1. Federal education money is denied states that don't allow prayer in public buildings.

2. Federal money may not be used to buy

textbooks or other educational materials that belittle the traditional role of women in society.

3. A tax exemption of $1,000 is allowed a household which includes a dependent person age 65 or over.

4. College students may not receive food stamps.

5. A corporation may deduct from taxes its contributions to a joint employee-employer day care facility.

6. Right of Religious Institutions. Federal agencies may not regulate religious activities such as church schools, religious homes and other ministries.

7. Contributions by an employed person to a savings account for his non-working spouse are tax deductible, up to $1,500 per year.

8. The current "marriage tax," which penalizes married couples with two incomes, is eliminated.

9. Legal Services Corporation money may not be used: (a) to compel abortions; (b) for school desegregation litigation; (c) for divorce litigation; and (d) for homosexual rights litigation.

Some conservatives may ask, "Is such a far-reaching piece of legislation really necessary? Doesn't it go against the conservative philosophy by trying to legislate morality and the American family?"

My quick and firm answer to the first question is, "Yes, the Family Protection Act is urgently needed because of all the liberal anti-family legislation and other actions over the last two decades."

And my answer to the second question is, "No, the Family Protection Act is not anti-conservative because conservatives believe that 'he who pays the piper should call the tune.' If taxpayer funds are used their elected representatives ought to be able to determine how such funds shall be used.''

Frankly, nothing shows more clearly the sharp difference between the New Right and what might be called the old right than the Family Protection Act.

In the past, conservatives concentrated almost always on resisting liberal anti-family actions.

In contrast, the Family Protection Act of Senator Paul Laxalt is an across-the board, indepth omnibus bill which has already thrown the liberals off-balance and will significantly strengthen the American family.

How needed is the Laxalt Act? Let me give you just a few examples of what the liberals have done to our way of life since the early 1960's.

• In 1962 and 1963, the Supreme Court held that voluntary prayer or Bible reading in the public schools violated the U.S. Constitution.

• Lyndon Johnson's Elementary and Secondary Education Act of 1965 began, in the words of House Education and Labor Committee staffer Lawrence Uzzel, "a massive shift of decisionmaking power" away from parents and local school boards to teacher unions and state and federal bureaucracies."

• In the mid-1960's, sociologist James S. Coleman authored a massive study which was widely used to justify busing to bring about school desegregation.

• In March 1972, Congress sent the Equal Rights Amendment to the states by an overwhelming majority.

• The January 1973 decision of the Supreme Court made abortion on demand the law of the land.

• Throughout the 1970's, there was an increasing legal trend toward decriminalization of marijuana with a resulting increase in the use of all drugs, especially among young people. According to the U.S. Surgeon General, by 1976, 60% of the 18-25 year-old group had used marijuana. 20% had "graduated" to harder drugs.

• The creation of the Department of Education in 1979 will further extend federal control over education.

Do we need the Laxalt Family Protection Act? You bet we do.

One of the latest attempts of the Federal government to intrude itself into the affairs of the family is the proposed Domestic Violence Act.

There's no denying that violence within the family is on the rise. The FBI reports that in 1978, 19% of the 19,555 people murdered in the U.S. were killed by a family member. Half of these involved the killing of one spouse by another.

Domestic violence, as Sen. Orrin Hatch has commented, affects all families—urban and rural, rich and poor, civilian and military. The victims are usually women who need protection for themselves and their children.

The liberals, typically, have come up with a new totally federal answer to this serious problem—the Domestic Violence Prevention and Services Act. The bill would create an OSHA-type agency. It would make all state and local jurisdictions answerable to a new Washington bureaucracy—the Federal Interagency Council on Domestic Violence.

As Senator Hatch has said, "This bill is one giant step by the federal social service bureaucracy into family matters which are properly, effectively and democratically represented in the state and local communities."

I agree with the Senator that most Americans do not want this new bureaucracy. Most Americans want a reduction and not an increase in federal interference and control. I believe that we can best help reduce violence in families by such things as:

1. Stopping inflation, the primary cause of mothers having to work outside of the home and leave their children with government social workers.

Inflation also causes many families to go heavily into debt which leads to family arguments, disputes and fights.

2. Getting illegal drugs out of the schools and communities.

3. Changing the minimum wage so that young people can get a job, develop responsibility, learn a trade and get off the streets.

4. Getting prayer back in the schools.

5. Removing sex and violence from TV, movies and magazines.

The very liberals who want more government programs and tax money to try and solve the problem of violence in the family do not seem to want to lift a finger to have the government get the massive amount of violence off of the TV programs flooding the average American home for 4-6 hours each and every day.

Another Federal "reform" in the works is Sen. Edward Kennedy's bill to rewrite the federal criminal code. But as *Conservative Digest* has reported, the bill would:

• Make it harder to prosecute smut peddlers, prostitutes, gangsters and drug traffickers.

• Permit the Federal hiring of unqualified people or people who pose a threat to national security.

• Send Americans to jail for throwing out government officials who are conducting unlawful inspections of their homes and factories. Under this provision, Bill Barlow, the brave Idaho businessman who refused to let an OSHA inspector conduct a warrantless search of his plant, would probably be in jail now. (See Chapter 9.)

• Make it virtually impossible to prosecute a union for any type of extortion.

• Tighten gun control laws.

Said *CD* of Kennedy's mammoth 440-page bill, the "changes lay the groundwork for the most significant expansion of federal power this country has seen, given half an inclination by the federal courts to interpret them as Kennedy has intended."

The Kennedy bill is exactly the kind of liberal legislation this country does not need and which the New Right is determined to stop.

And then there is the 1980 White House Conference on Families—an event organized, as New Right leader JoAnn Gasper has said, to drum up support for more federal spending, more federal regulations, and more political power for "alternative lifestyle" groups like homosexuals and women's libbers.

When pro-family forces won delegate contests in Oklahoma, Minnesota, Virginia and Maryland in late 1979 and early 1980, the liberals panicked.

Many states which had planned to elect most of their delegates changed their plans so that most delegates were appointed by the governors rather than elected. The governors, influenced by state steering committees usually controlled by liberals, appointed mostly liberal delegates to the conference.

Two conservative governors, Democrat Fob James of Alabama and Republican Otis Bowen of Indiana, decided not to cooperate with Jimmy Carter's attempted propaganda boost for more government involvement in family matters. Both Gov. James and Gov. Bowen declined to send delegates from their states.

The liberals' rhetoric was disgraceful. Delegates who opposed the Conference's anti-family bias were called "radical," "extremists" and "bigots."

The worst fears of the pro-family forces were realized at the June 1980 eastern regional meeting of the White House Conference on Families in Baltimore when the mostly appointed delegates endorsed the "right" to abortion, the Equal Rights Amendment, nondiscrimination against homosexuals, national health insurance and a guaranteed annual income of $13,000 for a family of four.

Many of the Pro-Family Coalition, led by New Right leaders Connie Marshner and Virginia state legislator Larry Pratt, walked out of the Baltimore meeting in protest. They refused to be part of such a Big Brother approach to the problems of the American family. As did the Catholic bishops of America after first agreeing to participate.

Dr. V. Dallas Merrell, president of the United Families of America, has set forth what he and other New Right groups want from the federal government.

• American families do not want guaranteed annual incomes—they want lower taxes and relief from inflation.

• American families do not want more but fewer welfare programs and a corresponding reduction in government spending. Federal spending eats into the family's income, forcing mothers to go to work to pay for food, clothing, shelter and other family basics.

• American families do not want national health insurance which drives up the cost of hospitals and doctors (as Medicare and Medicaid have done), but tax incentives so that families can choose their own form of private health care.

In a statement given to the White House Conference on Families, Dr. Merrell stressed that his organization welcomed such innovations as "flexitime," which permits mothers and fathers to better manage their time at home; increased use of computer terminals and telecommunications to allow more adult work at home; recreational and education opportunities at the neighborhood and community level rather than the citywide level.

Summed up Dr. Merrell:

"Government should get out of the way of the traditional family and should stop searching for 'alternatives' to it. We believe that the family is the basic unit of our society. As G.K.

Chesterton said, 'As are families, so is society.' "

But as we've seen, it is almost impossible for liberals to keep their hands off any part of our society—including its basic unit, the family.

In the December 1979 issue of *Ms.* magazine, Gloria Steinem published what Paul Weyrich called, "a blueprint for destroying the family." Encouraged by the spread of abortion, homosexuality, ERA, drugs and other anti-family factors, Steinem wrote that "we are now ready for more institutional, systematic change in the 1980's

The liberals, Paul says, plan to paint those who believe in traditional values "as a reactionary minority" trying to impose its outmoded ideas on the rest of society.

Well, we are *not* a reactionary minority but a traditional majority seeking to preserve American society as we have always known it.

However, I have to say I am disappointed to see so much of conservatives' energies spent on the "Thou Shalt Nots" of the Old Testament.

Of course I believe in the Thou Shalt Nots, but I also believe in the softness, gentleness and love of Christ. And I know that most all of my conservative friends do also, but many times the public doesn't see it.

For example, I share conservatives' disapproval of homosexuality. It is wrong and I want to do what I can to keep it from being considered as an acceptable alternative life style.

But I would like to see conservatives show as great or even a greater interest in opposing premarital sex and adultery.

Pre-marital sex and adultery, in my view, are much more serious threats to our society than homosexuality. They lead to over half a million illegitimate births a year and the break up of millions of marriages and broken homes for tens of millions of children.

There's another crisis in the American family today—our public schools.

Dan Alexander, president of the Mobile, Ala., board of education and an upcoming New Right leader, decided in 1978 that one answer was competency tests for teachers. The results were dramatic and revealing: only about half of the Mobile applicants who took the competency test in 1979 passed.

Alexander started a national movement. Some form of teacher testing has been approved in 12 states. Proposals for teacher testing have been introduced or are pending in nine other states. Polls show that 85% of U.S. adults favor teacher testing.

Here are some other needed reforms:

• A tightening up of standards in the education programs at the 1,150 colleges that train teachers.

• An abandoning of educational fads like the new Math, the "open classroom," and the look-say approach to reading (rather than the more effective "phonics" method).

• Better and more balanced textbooks. Norma Gabler of Longview, Texas, a New Right leader, has long been the nation's leading advocate of balanced textbooks for public schools. Because Texas is such a big market for textbook publishers, Mrs. Gabler has forced several textbook companies to rewrite their texts for the entire country.

• Eliminating bureaucratic regulations that require teachers to deal with public health officials, social workers, insurance companies.

juvenile police, and even divorce lawyers (about child custody).

• Dealing more effectively with violence in schools. The Pennsylvania legislature, for example, is considering a bill that would make carrying a gun or knife in school a serious crime.

• Encouraging principals to be more decisive in managing their schools.

• Getting Parent-Teacher Associations to become more involved.

And most important of all:

• Understanding that teaching children to read and write and do sums correctly is not all that hard—unless you make it so.

Who and what is behind the anti-family movement? Weyrich lists the major ones as those who do not believe in God, hardcore socialists, economic opportunists eager to make a buck from pornography, abortion, etc., and women's libbers who want a different political and cultural order.

Who and what make up the pro-family movement? Let me mention some of the leaders:

Senators Jake Garn and Orrin Hatch of Utah, Jesse Helms of North Carolina, Paul Laxalt of Nevada and Gordon Humphrey of New Hampshire; Congressmen John Ashbrook of Ohio, Robert Bauman of Maryland, Philip Crane of Illinois, Robert Dornan of California, Henry Hyde of Illinois, Larry McDonald of Georgia, and Bob Walker of Pennsylvania.

Bill Billings, National Christian Action Coalition; Dr. Bob Billings, The Moral Majority; JoAnn Gasper; attorney William Ball; Fr. Virgil C. Blum, S.J., Catholic League for Religious and Civil Rights; Harry Covert, editor, *Moral*

Majority Report; and Lottie Beth Hobbs, Pro-Family Forum.

Margaret Hotze, Life Advocates; June Larson, Citizens for Constructive Education; Ron Marr, *Christian Inquirer*; Rosemary Thomson, Family America, Martha Rountree, Leadership Foundation; Wayne Allen, Briarcrest Baptist School System (Memphis); and John Beckett, Intercessors for America.

Tim and Beverly LaHaye; Paige Patterson, Criswell Institute of Biblical Studies (Dallas); Ross Rhoads, Calvary Presbyterian Church (Charlotte); LaNeil Wright, Esther Action Council; Fr. Morton Hill, S.J., Morality in Media, and Fletcher Brothers, Gates Community Chapel (Rochester, N. Y.).

Randy Engel, U. S. Coalition for Life; Nellie Gray, March for Life; Patrick A. Trueman, Americans United for Life; and Ohio State Sen. Donald E. (Buz) Lukens, Americans for Life.

I deliberately did not mention such outstanding people as Jerry Falwell, Pat Robertson, James Robison, Howard Phillips, Phyllis Schlafly, and others whom I have discussed elsewhere in this book.

As far as the New Right and the entire pro-family movement are concerned, the lines have been drawn.

We will work in Washington, in state capitals, in cities and towns, in schools and churches, everywhere that is necessary, to protect and preserve the American family as it has developed and evolved during our country's 200 year history.

As columnist Joseph Sobran has written, "The last stronghold of private freedom is the family."

XI

Blacks, Blue Collar Workers
and the New Right

The United States Constitution is a great document. It contains the basic law by which our nation is governed, and it has worked magnificently for more than 200 years.

But it is a fact that some of the original Thirteen Colonies had strong doubts about the Constitution because they felt it did not adequately protect the rights of individuals.

That's why we have the Bill of Rights, the first 10 amendments to the Constitution, which spells out many specific rights of every individual citizen of the U.S.A. — and then reserves all other powers not mentioned in the Constitution to the states or the people.

Well, the liberals have been chipping away so furiously at our rights these past five decades that conservatives have been forced to stand up, not only for the original Bill of Rights, but for some new rights as well.

I'm talking about rights like:
- The Right to Work.
- The right to keep and bear arms (which is already in the Bill of Rights, but liberals try to overlook it).
- The Right to Life.
- The right to be safe in our homes and on our streets.
- The right not to have our money and assets reduced in value by government caused inflation.
- The right of our children to pray in school if they want to.
- The right to be secure from Communist subversion at home and Communist attack from abroad.

I want to make one very important point here. Conservatives are fighting for these basic rights not merely for ourselves but for all Americans.

One of the biggest lies of 20th century American politics is that liberals care about people and conservatives don't.

This is a bum rap put on us by liberals.

I suggest that it's conservatives who, by their actions, show real love and compassion for their fellow men.

And it's the liberals who seem to be able to close their eyes and turn their backs on the most massive outpouring of murder, slavery and crime ever known to man.

We should pray and work to help liberals understand how (1) their policies are responsible for turning Cambodia, Laos, Vietnam, parts of Africa and all of Eastern Europe over to the Communist slavemasters; (2) their policies of obsession with the rights of hardened criminals, drug pushers, the Mafia, and terrorists are primarily responsible for 141 violent crimes committed per hour in America.

If the liberals have such great love for their fellow man, what are their plans to help the 1.8 billion wretched souls held in slavery by the Communists, the tens of millions in America who are slaves to drugs and to welfare? Where are the liberals marching and demonstrating that something be done to stop one million violent crimes committed every year mostly against the minorities and senior citizens?

Those of us who are conservatives should hold our heads high and be proud of our record to help our fellow man.

By the way, this may come as a surprise to my friends and opponents.

I'm opposed to the death penalty. However, most of the New Right would probably disagree with me.

For most of my adult life I was an enthusiastic supporter of the death penalty as a means of preventing serious crime, such as murder, rape and kidnapping.

But in the past few years, I've come to see it differently. I now strongly oppose the death penalty.

I feel that executing 100 or 200 people a year is not going to make any real difference in the violent crime rate.

I believe that a strong case can be made that Christ would oppose the killing of someone as punishment for a crime.

Conservatives put a lot of energy into fighting for the death penalty, thinking that they're doing a lot to combat crime.

However, I feel that the most effective thing we can do to solve the crime problem is the swift and certain apprehension and jailing of those who commit crimes. And to give repeat, hardened criminals long jail sentences and not let them out after they've served a small fraction of their sentences.

A shocking 65% of those sent to jail commit another crime and are sent back to prison.

If we can keep most of the repeat offenders in jail for their full sentences, we'd probably reduce the crime rate by at least 50%. It seems so simple, you wonder why it's not done.

If you take a hardened repeat criminal who receives a 25 year sentence for murder, rape and robbery and keep him in jail for 25 years instead of letting him out in six years, you will be performing an act of mercy for the 10, 20 or 50 potential future victims of this criminal.

As I've said, the liberals' feelings about the New Right are very emotional and also often contradictory.

On the one hand, the left is beginning to see us as the wave of the future.

The *Denver Post* reported after the 1978 A. D. A. meeting in Washington, D. C.: "Some delegates, in fact, seemed to wonder whether the struggle might be futile, whether the country has swung into so conservative a political orbit that liberals may be on the path the mastadons trod—to extinction."

"Another A.D.A. delegate said, 'We're getting our . . . kicked.'

"Still another delegate said, 'I think the world is changing—that people, including us, are not as sure of themselves as they were a few years ago.

" 'I have a feeling that the ball is now in their (ultra conservatives) court. They're the true believers.' "

On the other hand, in the past few years, we've seen a tremendous concerted attack by the left on the New Right.

They've become almost paranoid about us. Most all major liberal organizations have put out letters, pamphlets and brochures attacking us. The AFL-CIO has produced a $70,000 film attacking the New Right.

When they attack us publicly, they take the approach that what we're doing must be immoral, illegal, dishonest, un-American, etc.

But when they meet and talk among themselves, they admit and acknowledge that they should learn from us, that they should begin to duplicate what we are doing.

But in public, it's usually a different matter.

At a September 1978 meeting of the AFL-CIO, William Winpisinger, president of the International Association of Machinists and Aerospace Workers, accused the New Right of being racist, fanatic, and fascist.

Winpisinger said, "Like its spiritual predecessors in Hitler's Germany, Mussolini's Italy and Franco's Spain, this army of the radical right has nothing but contempt for democracy and democratic institutions."

He called conservative columnists James J. Kilpatrick and William F. Buckley, Jr., "intellectual prostitutes." He described New Right leader Phyllis Schlafly as a "rich bitch from Illinois."

A COPE pamphlet distributed at this conference described me as "the godfather of the New Right," which "nourishes, grows and funds itself on a diet of extreme antiunionism."

As so often, Paul Weyrich put the AFL-CIO's attack on the New Right in perspective:

"They are defeating themselves," he told *Conservative Digest*. "Their criticism is so all-inclusive that they are causing people to look closely at what big labor leadership is all about."

As Paul pointed out, this kind of emotional attack is typical when an organization is losing ground and losing contact with its membership.

According to the University of Michigan, 69% of workers believe that union officials do what is best for themselves — not what is best for union members.

The New Right is working hard to separate the very different concerns of the AFL-CIO officials in Washington from those of union leaders and members in cities and towns across the country.

That's why a group of us met with local union leaders in Youngstown, Ohio, in February 1978. Among the New Right leaders who attended were Congressmen Phil Crane of Illinois and Mickey Edwards of Oklahoma, Howard Phillips, Paul Weyrich, John Buckley, then chairman of YAF and now a Virginia state legislator, myself and others.

It was an eye-opening experience for many of us. As Mickey Edwards said, "Those guys made some of us conservatives sound like moderates in comparison."

The Youngstown union officials were angry about Federal regulations, federal controls and just generally upset at the Federal government's involvement in their local community's business.

In response, Phil Crane began putting together a legislative package emphasizing such "lunch-pail" features as:

- A reinvestment tax credit to encourage industries to remain in the cities.
- Amendments to federal environmental laws that would delay the installation of costly antipollution equipment.

What we found out in Youngstown was that American workers are becoming increasingly conservative while the leadership of organized labor is becoming increasingly liberal.

In fact, I feel strongly that union officials, especially national union officials, do not represent their members on such issues as:

- The Panama Canal.
- Extension of time to ratify ERA.
- Increased welfare.
- The Department of Education
- Forced school busing.
- Food stamps.
- The war on poverty.

No wonder unions are losing membership. Their leadership is totally out of touch with the men and women they're supposed to represent.

George Wallace proved in his Presidential campaigns that the blue-collar worker in America is right of center and anti-Communist. But a 1980 study by Dr. Dan C. Heldman and Deborah L. Knight revealed that union PACs heavily back anti-national defense candidates.

According to their report, from 63% to nearly 71% of the campaign money of six large union PACs is spent in support of "anti-national security" candidates. However, only 7% to nearly 16% is contributed to "pro-national security" condidates and the remainder (19.7% to 24.9%) goes to the "middle."

A 1977 study by *The New Right Report* found that 96.2% of the AFL-CIO's COPE contributions to challengers in 1976 was spent *against* incumbents who scored 70% or higher on the National Security Index of the American Security Council. And 51.3% of the political contributions of the International Ladies Garment Workers Union to incumbents went to congressmen and senators scoring 10% or less on the National Security Index.

Conservative Mickey Edwards, who received 75% of the union vote in his 1978 Congressional campaign, summed up the widening gap between national union leaders and union members:

"When union people become the suburban working class, their concerns change. . . They're worried about inflation, the cost of groceries, and sending their kids to college. . .

"What the unions are still supporting is the great range of social programs, a consumer protection agency, Equal Rights Amendment, and so forth. The average rank-and-file member doesn't care about those issues."

Which brings me to the question of the relationship between the conservative movement and minorities, especially blacks.

When I'm asked why should a black be a conservative, my answer is:

1. Because conservatives (not liberals) are determined to get drugs out of the black schools and neighborhoods.

2. Because conservatives (not liberals) are determined to put those who are terrorizing

black neighborhoods with muggings, robbery, rape and murder in jail for very long periods of time.

Liberals seem obsessed with getting the criminal back into the neighborhood to try and reform him. Conservatives are committed to making the neighborhood safe for the remaining 98%.

3. Because conservatives (not liberals) are trying to make welfare a safety net for those who truly can't help themselves. Liberals, if there were no conservatives in Congress, would probably expand welfare to include most blacks, and they would raise the payments so high that there would be no incentive for them to ever get off welfare.

4. Because it's conservatives (not liberals) who would by making black neighborhoods safe from crime and drugs make sure that business and industry will return to black neighborhoods. And jobs will be available close to where blacks live, not 20-30 miles away.

5. Because it's conservatives (not liberals) who would demand that our public schools teach black children how to read, write and add so they can get good jobs and go to good colleges. Conservatives would demand that trouble-making students be kept out of school so teachers can teach and students can learn.

6. Because it's conservatives (not liberals) who would lower the minimum wage for young people. Unemployment among black youths was 36.5% in 1979, according to the Department of Labor, and is probably approaching 45% in 1980. If the minimum wage were $2.25 instead of $3.10, hundreds of thousands of black youths

who have no job experience or skills could get a job, get off welfare and the streets and learn a trade and become productive, tax paying and proud members of their community.

7. Because conservatives (not liberals) are demanding more growth in the private sector. It's the liberals (Jimmy Carter, Jerry Brown, Teddy Kennedy, etc.) who are telling American blacks that the American dream of opportunity and upward-mobility is over—that we must tighten our belts and do with less.

Why is it that the upper class, college educated blacks, such as Andy Young, Carl Rowan and Benjamin Hooks are obsessed with Rhodesia and South Africa? Where are the black leaders who are talking about the real problems of blacks?

Someday an American black is going to become a great leader of his people by pointing out that those blacks they thought were kings had no clothes on all this time.

This future American black leader will demand that schools teach black children and that disruptive children be expelled. He will demand that black neighborhoods be made safe from murder, robbery, rape and illegal drugs.

This black American will point out how most black leaders of the past 30 years have led blacks down a path of slavery, deceit and poverty.

It's white and black liberals who are the modern day Simon Legrees. It's the liberals with their dark ages ideas who would put blacks into bondage to the slave master called big government.

J. A. Parker, the black president of the Lincoln Institute and editor of *The Lincoln Review*, says:

"The billions of dollars of government money are no longer there. The well is almost dry at the federal level. The answer lies in more productivity, more growth and more jobs."

Margaret Bush Wilson, chairman of the NAACP, agrees, and has firmly stated her opposition to the liberals' no growth in energy philosophy. Said Mrs. Wilson of Jimmy Carter's 1977 less-energy plan:

The program was drawn up by people "who subscribe to a limits of growth philosophy" which would "freeze people to whatever rung of the economic ladder they happen to be on. That's okay if you're a highly educated 23-year old making $50,000 a year as a Presidential advisor. It's utter disaster if you're unskilled, out of work, and living in a ghetto."

XII

We're Ready to Lead

As the Bible says, there is a time for everything under heaven — a time to be born, and a time to die; a time to break down, and a time to build up; a time to keep silence, and a time to speak; a time of war, and a time of peace.

I think it is a time to lead.

Perhaps if I had been in the foxholes for 30 years as a lot of conservatives have, if I had been shot at and shelled and torn apart and suffered the defeats they have, I might have a defeatist attitude too.

But that's not the attitude of the New Right. We believe that we will prevail.

Several years ago, Phyllis Schlafly asked Dr. Fred Schwarz what did he think was the Communists' greatest asset, and before he could reply Phyllis answered her own question. She said she felt the Communists' greatest asset was their total conviction that they will win.

There isn't a Communist leader in the world worth his salt who doesn't feel that Communism is the wave of the future.

What leader of a major free world country believes in and talks about freedom being the wave of the future? Not one free world leader.

That's what conservatives have going for them now. New Right conservatives believe that we will govern America. And we believe that freedom is the wave of the future.

A lot of the older conservatives did not see themselves as winning and governing America. They saw themselves as sometimes influencing those who governed, but they did not see themselves as governing.

We see ourselves as winners. We are totally convinced that we have the ability to govern and we *will* govern in the not too distant future.

I have tried to suggest in this book what programs and policies conservatives might put into effect when they come to power concerning critical problems like national defense, taxes, education, government waste and spending, morality, the family, Big Government, Big Labor and Big Business and others. Some of the ideas have been my own. Many more have come from the rapidly increasing number of conservative experts in every part of our society.

For example, in foreign policy, we would:

(1) Build up our military forces regardless of the cost so that we are once again the Number One military power in the world. Every nation in the world — except the Soviet Union and other Communist countries — would be relieved, publicly or privately, when we did.

A national Sindlinger poll, taken in May 1980, showed that nearly 8 out of every 10 Americans (77.1%) feel the nation "should spend whatever is necessary to meet national security objectives."

(2) React decisively to Communist aggression by diplomatic and where necessary military means. The invasion of Afghanistan demanded more than a boycott of the Olympics and half-hearted sanctions.

At the very least, a conservative President would have done the following:

• Immediately halted *all* grain, technology, computer equipment, etc. on their way to Russia or Russian satellite countries. In contrast, Carter allowed present contracts on grain shipments to be sent to Russia, and we are still selling grain to Communist countries such as East Germany.

• Stopped all credit and loans to Soviet Russia by the Department of Commerce, the Export-Import Bank and all other federal agencies.

• Closed our embassy in Moscow and closed the Soviet embassy here in Washington, D.C.

• Put SALT II on the back burner, permanently.

(3) Treat our allies as friends and our enemies as enemies.

We seem to spend more time courting enemies like Communist China than friends like Taiwan.

(4) Strengthen our alliances not only with Western Europe and Japan, but with key nations in South America, Africa, the Middle East and Asia.

(5) Build a military presence with our allies in those areas where we are most needed — in the Eastern Mediterranean, the Arabian Sea and the Persian Gulf — areas close to Africa and the Middle East which remain the most vulnerable to the Soviets.

(6) Reduce U.S. support of the United Nations. Why should the United States with 6% of the world's population pay 25% while Russia with 7% of the world's population pays only 10% and Communist China with 20% of the world's population pays only 5% of the U.N. budget?

(7) Take the chains off the CIA, the Defense Intelligence Agency and the National Security Agency that were put on them by liberal Senators and Congressmen.

(8) Spend at least as much of our time and national energy trying to undermine totalitarian regimes in Communist countries as they spend trying to undermine freedom inside the U.S.

In his brilliant book, *Strategy of Survival*, British journalist-historian Brian Crozier argues that it is essential to realize that the enemy is internal as well as external.

(1) Crozier suggests an extraordinary session of NATO to coordinate counter-subversion and counter-action against terrorism.

(2) He proposes the creation of a "Department of Unconventional War" at NATO headquarters.

(3) He calls for an immediate ending of credits for and exports of technology to the USSR.

(4) He urges a massive expansion of information and propaganda, with special attention to

improving Radio Free Europe, Radio Liberty and other overseas facilities.

Peter Osnos, national editor of the *Washington Post*, confirmed the importance of Radio Free Europe and the Voice of America, writing on June 13, 1980:

"There is no way to overstate the importance of these stations in informing tens of millions of people in the Soviet Union and Eastern Europe about what is going on around the globe and in their own countries. These stations amount to the injection of a free press in lands in which there otherwise is none."

In economic policy, we would:

(1) Reduce federal spending either by constitutional amendment or law, tying the size of the annual federal budget to the annual GNP.

(2) Significantly reduce personal and business taxes.

(3) Balance the budget — and set aside a certain percentage each year for reduction of the national debt, now approaching $1 trillion.

(4) Reduce and decentralize the bureaucracy. Congressman Crane has suggested that various federal departments could be dispersed around the nation. Move the Agriculture Department to Iowa, Interior to Alaska, Commerce to Chicago. With today's instantaneous communications, bureaucrats could still talk with each other, but decentralization would help check the growing momentum of big government, and bring government in contact with the people it serves.

(5) Balance our exports and imports by demanding that foreign markets be open to American goods — or American markets will be closed to foreign goods.

(6) Reduce the paperwork, regulations and red tape which cost businesses — especially small businesses — and consumers more than $100 billion a year.

(7) Lower business taxes to encourage companies to modernize equipment, create new jobs and become more competitive in today's international markets.

(8) Make America energy self-sufficient by (a) decontrolling all oil and natural gas; (b) asking utility companies where possible to switch to coal; (c) suspend those environmental regulations that discourage the exploration of alternative sources of energy; (d) open up public lands for the new exploration of oil and natural gas; (e) change federal regulations so that nuclear power plants can be built in 5 or 6 years instead of the 13 years the government now requires.

(9) Limit judicial power to enforcing the law, not creating policy.

In all things, we must encourage a climate of freedom and experimentation so that men and women can reap the fruits of their labor, either by their hands or their heads.

In social policy, we would:

(1) Abolish the Department of Education, which seeks to displace both the local boards of education and parents as the final judge of our children's education.

(2) Let the Equal Rights Amendment die a well-deserved death.

(3) Approve a constitutional amendment protecting the Right to Life from the moment of conception.

(4) Approve a constitutional amendment forbidding the use of busing for the purposes of desegregation — a move favored by the overwhelming majority of black *and* white parents.

(5) End the use of quotas in education and employment.

(6) Retain the loan, work study and scholarship programs for students who attend college — but insure that all such loans are repaid in full. (See Chapter 9).

(7) Free the FBI of liberal imposed regulations that prevent it from effectively protecting the domestic peace and internal law and order.

In moral policy, we would:

(1) Restore prayer to the nation's public schools.

In the latest nationwide Gallup poll, released in May 1980, 76% of those surveyed said they favor a constitutional amendment to permit voluntary prayers in public schools.

(2) Keep the tax-exempt status of private school⁻

(3) Pressure the major TV networks and advertisers to eliminate the sexual and immoral programs which fill almost every hour of prime time Monday through Sunday.

(4) Work for the passage of Sen. Paul Laxalt's Family Protection Act — legislation which is pro-family, pro-God and a reaffirmation of the traditions and morals on which this nation was built.

(5) Wage an all-out war against pornography and immorality. Specific actions could include (a) local zoning laws prohibiting pornographic book stores and massage parlors, (b) strict enforcement of laws against prostitutes *and* their

clients, (c) strict enforcement of laws against interstate transportation of porno movies and books, and (d) a coordinated, concentrated campaign by the Justice Department against the major source of all of the above — organized crime.

Such reforms will not come easily. They will need the backing of the highest authorities in the land.

That is why I recommend that the next President of the United States create a National Commission to Restore America — made up of a volunteer group of our most distinguished conservative citizens who would report to the President, Congress and the American people about the critical challenges confronting us, and how we can best overcome them.

I say "conservative citizens" because for almost 50 years this country has suffered from mostly liberal commissions, liberal legislation and liberal policies, all of them administered by liberals. The result has been that liberals have brought America to its knees financially, morally, militarily and educationally.

It's time to give the majority of Americans — the conservatives — an opportunity to try and get us out of the chaos the liberals got us into.

The National Commission could be headed by a distinguished American such as Bill Simon, Paul Laxalt, Jack Kemp, Richard DeVoss, or Bill Armstrong. It would be required to complete its work and report to the President no later than one year after he became President.

It would be far more than an updated version of the Hoover Commission of the 1940's, as good and as needed as that commission was.

The National Commission to Restore America would offer a conservative "Agenda for the 1980's and 1990's" — an agenda by which every American could attain the American dream.

The National Commission would include men and women who have shown that they can solve problems. There are many conservatives who can talk about how bad a situation is, but only those who have demonstrated they can build, turn things around, and successfully solve massive problems, should be appointed.

In other words, most of the Commission's key people should come from the private sector.

I think Reagan has the right idea when he says that the people in his administration will be "people who don't want a job in government. I want people that will have to step down to a position in government."

I feel strongly that those who have shown they are good at speech making and shaking hands but have no demonstrated ability in the area of administration should not be trusted with solving America's massive problems.

Many people think because someone is well-known, makes a great speech and never forgets a name or face, that he is qualified to lead.

That's like saying the airline's best pilot should run the airline, the hospital's best brain surgeon should run the hospital, or a Pulitzer Prize writer should be the president of the publishing company.

The skills necessary to discuss a problem are different than the skills to solve the problem.

God seldom gives one person the talents of being a great speaker, writer, motivator and administrator. Two rare 20th century examples would be Douglas MacArthur and Winston Churchill.

The National Commission would not deal in splendid generalities but would present specific recommendations, like those suggested in this book, that would bring about an economic, military and spiritual rebirth in America.

I have no doubts whatsoever that together we can come up with the answers to restore and revitalize America.

I'm thinking of proposals like:

• Sen. Jesse Helms' 1978 bill, entitled, "The Taxpayers' Bill of Rights Act," which sets forth the taxpayer's rights with regard to the IRS.

Among other things, the act would (1) require IRS agents to inform the taxpayer of his right to counsel, his right to remain silent and that any statement made might be used against him; (2) provide for the government to pay attorney's fees in cases won by the taxpayer; (3) set up an Assistant Commissioner for Taxpayer Services to act as an ombudsman within IRS for the people; and (4) authorize the GAO to audit regularly the efficiency and fairness of the IRS.

• Prof. Walter Williams' proposal to (1) exempt young people from the full requirements of the minimum wage law, (2) modify national labor law to allow free access to jobs, (3) reduce job licensing and business regulations, (4) provide ways for delivering higher quality education.

If we take these steps, argues Prof. Williams, a distinguished black economist:

"Today's disadvantaged minorities will melt into the economic mainstream *en masse*, as have other disadvantaged minorities — minorities fortunate enough to have become urbanized before America had so many laws that cut the bottom rungs off the economic ladder."

We can certainly put back the first rung by adopting Professor Williams' suggestion to exempt young people from the minimum wage.

I referred earlier to the importance of the Voice of America and Radio Free Europe in getting the truth to people behind the Iron Curtain. Alexander Solzhenitsyn, the great Russian author, Nobel Laureate and former inmate of the Gulag, makes the critical point that it is not enough to increase the amount of programming. The *content* of the programming must improve, too, and drastically.

In the spring 1980 issue of *Foreign Affairs*, Solzhenitsyn charged that the daily programs of the Russian section of the Voice of America are "filled with trite and inconsequential drivel which can do nothing but irritate the hungry and oppressed millions of listeners whose paramount need is to be told the truth about their own history."

Hours of radio time, according to the Nobel laureate, are filled with reports about beer bottles, ocean cruises, and American pop singers.

"In their zeal to serve detente," Solzhenitsyn wrote, "(the directors of the Voice of America) remove everything from their programs which might irritate the communists in power." The VOA, for example, limited coverage of Solzhenitsyn's statement on the arrest of dissident leader Alexander Ginsburg in 1977 to one sentence.

Conservatives are convinced, as are dissidents like Solzhenitsyn, Alexander Ginsburg, Vladimir Bukovsky, Alexander Maximov, and Yuri Orlov, that those of us who have freedom must forge ever closer links with the captive peoples of the communist world. Otherwise, as Solzhenitsyn has written, "so much has been ceded, surrendered and traded away that today even a fully united Western world can no longer prevail."

Congressman Jack Kemp is probably best known for his proposal to cut income taxes 30% over the next three years. But he's also concerned about the total economic picture of the United States.

In his thoughtful book, *An American Renaissance*, the Congressman urges that:

• The welfarism that is killing off America's desire to work must be changed.

• Featherbedding and "make work" must be eliminated.

• New technology must be readily accepted.

• Incentives through lower taxation "must be the torch that relights the competitive spirit in all Americans."

In May 1980, Jack Kemp introduced in Congress still another creative approach to improving our economy — The Urban Jobs and Enterprise Zone Act, which would provide tax incentives for individuals and small businesses in the inner city.

Conservative ideas? We've got a million of them!

(1) Deregulate the trucking industry. Congress did get around to making a move in this direction in June 1980. The new law could save consumers up to $8 billion annually in transportation costs on the things they buy. But the law only affects the interstate trucking

236

companies which make up less than half the trucking industry.

(2) Repeal the Davis-Bacon Act, a long-out-of-date Depression law.

The act was intended to stop contractors from coming into an area and hurting the local construction industry by underbidding local builders for the work available there. It requires the Labor Department to determine the "prevailing wage" in an area and make contractors pay their workers at least that wage on any federal job.

But the Act has artificially increased wages, raised prices and caused inflation, and produced fewer construction-related jobs.

Contractor Jim Pizzagalli of Burlington, Vt., told the *Washington Star* in March 1979 that Davis-Bacon "artificially" sets wages "at a given rate. That rate generally tends to be the union rate, so you tend to get a small segment of the economy setting the wages for the entire market."

That's no way to run an economy that has the inflation-unemployment-recession problems ours has.

(3) Adopt an educational voucher system. Long recommended by Milton Friedman and others, such a system would give parents a tax deduction for what they spend to send their children to a private school.

(4) Do away with government licensing requirements. Such requirements reduce rather than increase the number of jobs. For example, New York City strictly limits the number of taxicab licenses, called medallions, to 11,577. These medallions may be bought and sold. As

of August, 1980, they were costing $64,000. The result is that any poor would-be taxi entrepreneur is frozen out of the taxi business.

In Washington, D.C., on the other hand, licensing requirements are kept to a minimum. As a result, the number of independent taxicabs is the largest in any major city in the country. And most of those taxicabs are minority-owned.

(5) Eliminate the present government monopoly in the delivery of first class mail.

Many reforms have been suggested and some have been made (like the use of the Zip code), but the Postal Service continues to be inefficient for one simple reason — it is a monopoly, a union-dominated, bureaucratic monopoly.

The success of UPS and other private carriers proves that it is possible to get mail and parcels from one city to another city in a reasonable amount of time for a reasonable price.

Unfortunately, the Post Office's usual response to competition has been to urge Congress and the courts to stop it.

Monopoly is the problem and again the solution is simple — break up the monopoly of the Postal Service by letting private corporations compete with the Post Office in the delivery of first class and other mail.

Yes, conservatives have a lot of good ideas to make America a better place to live and work in. But most importantly, what we of the New Right can offer is *leadership*.

I feel that most of the problems that the cause of freedom has in America and in the world today are because of a lack of leadership. Most of the problems in the world could be corrected if we had a few good leaders.

If you think about it, this country is here today because of a few dozen people. If there had been no Washington, no Franklin, no Jefferson, no Adams, plus 20 others some 200 years ago we might still be a colony of Great Britain.

Starting in the early 1930's, we did not graduate from the universities or colleges future conservative leaders.

For some reason, we conservatives skipped an entire generation of leaders.

As a result, in the 1950's, 1960's and 1970's the left had their Humphreys, Stevensons, Kennedys, Rockefellers, Javits, Mondales and Reuthers.

But the right had very few leaders during these three decades.

We did have a fair number of people who were well-known, articulate, good writers, good debaters, who had charisma.

And most people would think that they were leaders. But only in the last few years did I come to understand that most were spokesmen. They were not leaders.

A leader will make things happen, he will start a new organization or a new magazine. He will call meetings, suggest assignments, then call a follow-up meeting to review the progress.

A leader realizes that winners have plans and losers have excuses.

There is a big difference between a spokesman and a leader. It's not that a spokesman is not important; it's just that you need both spokesmen and leaders. But for many years conservatives had spokesmen but very few leaders.

But starting in the 1950's and early 1960's, we started to produce from our universities and colleges those who have gone on to provide the critically needed conservative leadership.

First came Bill Buckley, Bill Rusher, Stan Evans, and Phyllis Schlafly, then in rapid succession, Howard Phillips, Carol and Bob Bauman, Jesse Helms, Jerry Falwell, Jameson Campaigne, Orrin Hatch, Mickey Edwards, Paul Weyrich, James Robison, Morton Blackwell, Terry Dolan and many, many others.

While the conservative leadership gap is being filled, the liberals are rapidly losing their leadership. And it will be at least 10 years before the kids who were in the streets marching against the war in Viet Nam will be old enough to provide leadership for the left.

It appears to me that the 1980's will see the liberals suffering from a serious leadership gap.

This provides an enormous opportunity for the conservatives to take charge of the major institutions in America while the left is not playing with a full team.

However, we need lots more leaders and at all levels, not just in Washington, D.C.

I'd like *you*, personally, to give some serious thought to becoming a leader. You might think about becoming a candidate for the school board, city council, state legislature or Congress or perhaps you might seek a position in your local Democratic or Republican organization.

Don't sell yourself short by thinking you don't have the talent or ability or background to run for or hold public office.

Very few people who hold public office are genuine giants. They are people for the most part like you and me — engineers, housewives, doctors, concerned parents, salesmen.

Don't make the mistake of waiting for a committee of the leading citizens of your community to plead with you to run for Congress, or mayor, or city council, or the board of education.

Occasionally, it does work that way. But if Jimmy Carter had waited for a committee to plead with him, he'd still be waiting in Plains, Ga.

Orrin Hatch, a Salt Lake City attorney with no political experience, decided to make his plunge in 1976. He now represents Utah in the U.S. Senate.

Gordon Humphrey, an Allegheny Airlines co-pilot who had never run for public office, decided to provide some leadership in 1978. Gordon did not have the support of any big name New Hampshire political leaders, only his own friends, his associates from The New Hampshire Conservative Caucus and a few New Right national leaders. He now represents New Hampshire in the U.S. Senate.

There are many more Orrin Hatches and Gordon Humphreys in America — conservatives who can and must make a contribution now to their country.

For the past 50 years, conservatives have stressed almost exclusively economic and foreign policy. The New Right shares the same basic beliefs of other conservatives in economics and foreign policy matters, but we feel that conservatives can not become the dominant political force in America until we stress the issues of concern to ethnic and blue collar Americans, born-again Christians, pro-life Catholics and Jews.

Some of these issues are busing, abortion, pornography, education, traditional Biblical moral values, and quotas.

However, there are certain qualities that the New Right has that previous conservatives didn't have.

As a general rule, New Right conservatives are usually in their 20's, 30's or 40's (with some exceptions, such as Jesse Helms). They are aggressive, sharp, tough, work long hours, meet often, develop strategy, plans and tactics, cooperate with Democrats, Independents and Republicans, use and understand new technology. Their day is filled with activities designed to replace liberals with conservatives in all major American institutions.

They are conservatives who are tired of losing and are personally committed to bringing freedom to America and the world in the near future. And they have a firm conviction that they will succeed.

What keeps conservatives like Jesse Helms, that dedicated, tireless "conscience of the Senate," going? He has the following motto on a plaque in his Senate office, and I've adopted it as a guide for my life:

"God does not require me to succeed, but He does require me to try."

Frankly, I think He requires all of us to try.

As I said at the very beginning of this book, the left is old and tired. We on the New Right are young and vigorous.

Many of the liberals' leaders like Adlai Stevenson, Nelson Rockefeller, Hubert

Humphrey, Robert and Jack Kennedy are gone. Our leaders are coming into their own.

The liberals had a lot of victories over the last 50 years. But they've grown soft and sluggish. They have lost confidence in themselves and in their ideas.

We're lean, determined and hungry — to gain victories for conservatism and to renew our great country.

Yes, the tide is turning. It is turning our way — freedom's way.

Appendix A

WHAT THE PRESS SAYS
ABOUT THE NEW RIGHT

"The aim of the New Right is nothing less than creating a conservative middle-class majority in American politics. Republicans, of course, have talked for years of finding some elusive conservative majority; but political professionals don't dismiss the New Right effort lightly because these conservative activists, who care little about party labels, have the money, the know-how and the issues to make an impact in American politics. . ."

James P. Gannon,
The Wall Street Journal

"The list of issues on which conservatives are forming these ad hoc coalitions is broad and varied—including, although not limited to, the Panama Canal, the Equal Rights Amendment, abortion, pornography, right-to-work laws, the B-1 bomber, welfare, federal financing of elections, gun control, disarmament, common situs picketing, prayer in the schools, Cuba, school busing to achieve racial desegregation, abolition of the electoral college, the environment, revision of the labor law and China.

"By taking such an approach, the conservatives are essentially following the same strategy that made the liberal coalition in the Democratic Party the dominant force in our politics over the last several decades. . .

"The conservatives also have gained strength because their leaders, in most if not all cases, have become more pragmatic and less emotionally defensive about their causes."

Syndicated columnists Jack
Germond and Jules Witcover

"What they really are, generally speaking, is a group of anti-Establishment, middle-class political rebels more interested in issues like abortion, gun control, busing, ERA, quotas, bureaucracy and the grassroots tax revolt than in capital gains or natural gas depletion."

> Syndicated columnist
> Kevin Phillips

"In legislative battles in Congress, in political fundraising, in mobilizing support on controversial issues throughout the country, in winning key off-year elections, and in sheer intellectual energy and talent, the New Right has overwhelmed the traditional Republican establishment."

> Saul Friedman, *St. Louis Globe Democrat*

"The New Right differs in organization, style and tactics from the 'Old Right' that supported Barry Goldwater in 1964. The new generation is more tightly organized, better financed, more sophisticated and more pragmatic than their predecessors. They are prepared to accept partial victories that the Old Right, with its kamikaze instincts, would have considered ideological defeat."

> *The New York Times*

"They are a new breed of Senate conservatives—younger, brighter and far more willing to compromise than most of their ideological predecessors in the Republican right wing. . . But members of the Senate's 'New Right' insist their time has come—and their growing influence has impressed colleagues on both sides of the aisle."

Newsweek

"Often outmaneuvered by the Left during the 1960s, the Right has now copied the enemy's tactics. Like COPE, the political arm of the AFL-CIO, the New Right has plunged into the grassroots, ringing doorbells, phoning and passing out leaflets."

Time

"The New Right (are) dedicated activists who have been making a name for themselves. . . by following a strategy that they think can lead to political control of the country. . ."

William Lanouette,
National Journal

"Senate liberals, already an endangered species after [1978's] election upsets, may go the way of the dodo if rightwing pressure groups join forces for a determined headhunting campaign. And there is evidence that they are doing just that."

Columnist Jack Anderson

"While Democrats and Republicans snipe away at each other from entrenched positions, a third force is quietly building a political apparatus that pointedly disregards party labels.

"The newcomers: conservatives of widely varying backgrounds, linked by a common devotion to limited government, free enterprise and a strong national defense.

"Their aim: mobilize public opinion on major issues and elect conservatives at every level, whether they run on Republican or Democratic tickets. . ."

U.S. News & World Report

"Keep an eye on the expanding New Right in U.S. politics. It crosses both big-party lines and poses headaches for each of them. GOP sees it as a financial rival since the New Right is raising millions through direct-mail pleas—money that the GOP might otherwise round up. Democrats are apprehensive because the bloc has been highly effective in working to torpedo bills supported by unions friendly to the Democrats. Labor's reaction? It has formed a special unit to combat the New Right."

*The U.S. News
Washington Letter*

"A political army of Christian crusaders is emerging from the religious New Right. They are groups of . . . fundamentalist church people who in the past have shunned political activism, holding that their mission was to win conversions for the Lord.

"Now, they are gearing up for a political showdown of their own.

"Most of them are closely aligned with prominent television evangelists and conservative members of Congress, and they have a potential constituency of an estimated minimum of 50 million evangelical conservatives."

The Dallas Morning News

"If the heart of the Christian voter campaign is in Middle America, its head is in Stanton Square (in Washington, D.C.).

"A onetime slum that is now a reviving neighborhood, this section of stern Victorian brick and stone townhouses is four blocks from the back of the U.S. Capitol.

"It houses a dozen or so organizations devoted to God and country. Most of them are involved in legislative lobbying on 'family issues' like abortion, homosexuality and prayer in public schools.

"But a few — Moral Majority, Christian Voice, and the National Christian Action Coalition — are out to win voters and influence Congress this year, turning out liberals and replacing them with those who think right."

The Atlanta Journal

"The new conservatives . . . are bound to be a serious threat to the established Senate Republican leadership, which has tended in recent years to be moderate and consensus-oriented . . . . the group may be able to apply substantial pressure from within the Senate toward their general goal of moving the Republican party to the Right . . . . conservatives may be striking a more responsive chord than usual, and they may be increasingly in a position to persuade the country to practice what they are preaching."

Sanford Ungar, contributing
editor, *The Atlantic*

"What has happened, in recent years, is that the so-called New Right has finally learned to use some time-honored techniques. It is particularly instructive to drop in on a Friday meeting of the new conservatives in a Capitol Hill office, where Paul Weyrich, the executive director of the Committee for the Survival of a Free Congress, may be heard discussing the latest congressional bills with a group including an editor of Richard Viguerie's publications, a spokesman for the anti-gun control people, a representative of the National Right to Work Committee and a few anti-Washington journalists.

"The spirit reminds one of New Deal days, when the White House aides Tommy Corcoran and Ben Cohen might be meeting with a follower of labor leader Walter Reuther and a few assorted employees from Henry Wallace's Department of Agriculture and Henry Morgenthau's Treasury to talk, say, of the chances of the Supreme Court packing bill.

"The difference, this time, is that smart young organizers such as Paul Weyrich tend to concentrate on so-called social issues where their New Deal predecessors were concerned primarily with economics. There are a lot of social 'single issues' to be combined into new Election Day coalitions."

Syndicated columnist
John Chamberlain

WHAT OUR OPPONENTS
ARE SAYING ABOUT US

"There's no question that the Right is getting increasingly successful on Capitol Hill."

> Vicki Otten, legislative
> representative, Americans
> for Democratic Action

"(We have) respect for the professional and effective way you're going about organizing politically . . . ."

> Ben Albert, director of
> public relations, COPE, in a
> letter to Committee for the
> Survival of a Free Congress

"The right wing is stronger, richer, and better organized than ever . . . . They're ready to give us a dose of our own medicine."

> The liberal National
> Committee for an
> Effective Congress

"In the whole question of political technology, the right is way ahead of the progressives."

> Lee Webb, executive
> director, Conference on
> Alternative State and Local
> Public Policy

"After listening more than an hour to a gloomy, late-night recitation of New Right techniques and tactics, one delegate to the 31st annual convention of Americans for Democratic

Action summed up in a single inelegant phrase: 'We're getting our --- kicked.'

"Another delegate said: 'Once we had it, but we lost it,' referring to the conservatives' apparent drive and zeal.

"'They're doing the same stuff we did in the civil rights day and in the Vietnam war days. But we don't do it anymore. I don't know where we lost it, but it's gone.'"

From a Denver Post article
in June 1978

"The only thing new about the New Right is its technique, sophistication and method of operation . . . . They develop to the nth degree the direct mail technique of raising money by computerizing mailing lists.

"They organize committees as mirror images of liberal committees. They have one that copies COPE. They have one that copies the National Committee for an Effective Congress, one that copies Common Cause, etc., except I think it's fair to say they have developed it to an even higher effectiveness than the liberals have."

Teacher's Voice

"They are bold, resourceful, well-organized and well-financed, and they are also deadly serious, true and passionate believers."

The Fear Brokers by former
Sen. Thomas McIntyre

"New Right leaders are not rabid crackpots or raving zealots. The movement they are building is not a lunatic fringe . . . . its strength is increasing almost daily . . . . Candidates elected by the New Right can reverse the U.S. political and social climate. Carefully selected, trained and briefed, (New Right) candidates — if elected — will work to defeat every social program that you and ADA support."

"A Citizen's Guide to the Right Wing," published by Americans for Democratic Action

"Rightwing political action organizations . . . are finding allies among the social conservatives within the Democratic Party — many who call themselves 'pro-family,' 'pro-life,' 'pro-decency,' those who seek to undermine public confidence in public education, and the anti-ERA and anti-gun-control activists.

"They begin with a base of support from among the economic conservatives in the Republican Party who are identified with the tax revolt and right-to-work movements and who favor greatly expanded defense spending. They are also wooing fundamentalist, 'born-again', and other vulnerable religious constituencies.

"The New Right organizations are extremely skilled in the use of computer technology and direct-mail fundraising. With sophisticated computer programs they can raise millions of dollars for political campaigns and deluge Congress with single-issue mail. They are also beginning to avail themselves of the funds being collected by the political action committees (PACs) of corporations."

Former Congressman Donald M. Fraser (D-Minn),

in a fundraising letter for
the Democrat-Farmer-Labor
Party
(Many political observers
credit a New Right-type
campaign with defeating
Fraser in his 1978 Senate
attempt.)

"But the New Right is far more pragmatic
and intelligent than the fringe conservative
movements of recent vintage. The people who
provide the New Right's ideas and political
leadership may be said to be extremist in the
sense that they would like to reorder society in
some pretty radical ways.

"But it would be a mistake to lump the New
Right under the general rubric of extremism. To
do so would be to treat this phenomenon less
seriously than it merits."

Arch Puddington, executive
director, League for
Industrial Democracy

"Collectively these new organizations have
created a centralized political action fundraising
capability that dwarfs any previous organized
attempts by the older conservative groups and
all of the current capability of the liberal
community."

Americans for Democratic
Action

"My undoing was started two years ago in the
suburbs of Washington by (conservative direct
mail specialist Richard) Viguerie and in the

suburbs of Los Angeles by the Reagan kitchen cabinet."

> Former Lt. Gov. Mervyn M.
> Dymally of California,
> explaining his 1978 loss to
> Republican Mike Curb

"Some political observers believe the New Right could become a powerful third political party with its own Presidential candidate by 1984."

> *Tennessee Teacher*,
> journal of the Tennessee
> Education Association

"The success of the New Right is due not only to its own ingenuity and luck, but also to the present defensiveness and confusion within the progressive community. While the New Right displays a boisterous elan, the progressive community is questioning most of its assumptions, including such basic ones as the value of political activism."

> Scott Wolf, in the ultra-
> liberal *Democratic
> Viewpoint*

"The right wing has been around a long time in many various forms, but it has become more sophisticated with time and experience and is now a substantial influence in American economics and politics."

> Wesley McCune in
> *Viewpoint*, quarterly
> magazine of Industrial
> Union Dept., AFL-CIO

Appendix B

Conservative Publications and Organizations

For those of you who want to get more involved in the conservative movement, I have put
together the following list of three major publications and five major organizations and PACs.

Conservative Digest (monthly)
7777 Leesburg Pike
Falls Church, V4 22043
Annual subscription: $15

Human Events (weekly)
422 First Street, S.E.
Washington, D.C. 20003
Annual subscription: $25

National Review (26 issues)
150 East 35th Street
New York, N.Y. 10016
Annual subscription: $24

American Conservative Union
Suite 400
316 Pennsylvania Avenue, S.E.
Washington, D.C. 20003

Committee for the Survival of a Free Congress
8 Library Court, S.E.
Washington, D.C. 20003

Conservative Victory Fund
422 First Street, S.E.
Washington, D.C. 20003

National Conservative Political Action
  Committee
Suite 513
1500 Wilson Boulevard
Arlington, VA 22209

The Conservative Caucus
422 Maple Avenue, East
Vienna, VA 22180

Appendix C

National Day of Prayer and Fasting
Petition to Elected Public Officials

We the undersigned do respectfully petition you, our elected leaders, to help bring America back to God by setting aside the Sunday before each Thanksgiving as a National Day of Fasting and Prayer.

Just as we celebrate the bounty of God's blessing on Thanksgiving Day with the traditional family meal, we will set aside the Sunday before Thanksgiving as a day of fast and prayer to bring us closer to God.

We will fast and pray as Jesus and Moses did, so that we will be strengthened to meet the many serious challenges facing our nation.

We will humbly pray that God lead our nation through the many dangers that lie ahead and to restore His blessing on the American people.

Many of our personal and national problems have developed because we have forgotten to thank God for our blessings, our opportunities, our freedoms and our great country.

_____
Name

_____
Address

_____
City, state & zip

_____
Name

_____
Address

_____
City, state & zip

Send copies of this petition to public officials such as mayors, city councilmen, governors, Congressmen.
(See other side.)

Name

Address

City, state & zip

Name

Address

City, state & zip

Name

Address

City, state & zip

Name

Address

City, state & zip

Name

Address

City, state & zip

Name

Address

City, state & zip

Send copies of this petition to public officials such as mayors, city councilmen, governors, Congressmen.

Index

Use this coupon and you get **8 FREE ISSUES OF**

the New Right report

The New Right Report:

- a 6 page newsletter
- mailed 1st class to your home twice a month
- published by Viguerie Communications Corporation
- reports on the plots, the plans, and the ploys of Republicans and Democrats, Conservatives and Liberals—with special emphasis on what is happening inside the New Right.

Our guarantee:

We will immediately refund the unused portion of your subscription if you are unsatisfied for any reason.

The New Right Report. 668 Independence Ave., Marion, Ohio 43302

☐ **Yes,** I want *The New Right Report* for one year (24 issues, regular price $36.00). But I'm enclosing only $24.00 for all 24 issues. The first 8 issues I get **FREE.**

☐ I also want to buy gift subscriptions to *The New Right Report* for my friends at the same great ⅓ off price. I've listed them on a separate paper.

Name _____

Address _____

City, State, Zip _____

Make checks payable to: The New Right Report
Payment must accompany order.

Order Form

THE NEW RIGHT:
WE'RE READY TO LEAD

By Richard A. Viguerie

Introduction by Jerry Falwell

Order quantity copies of *The New Right: We're Ready to Lead* for your organization, your church, your club, your school, your friends. This dynamic book is filled with ideas and programs that can make America the Number One military power in the world again . . . put prayer back in our schools. . . protect our great Judeo-Christian heritage. . . reduce waste in government. . . preserve the American family. . .help you to be a more effective citizen. It's a book that can help make America great again.

Quantity Prices

1-9 copies	$2.25	100-499 copies	$1.25
10-24 copies	$1.90	500 or more	
25-99 copies	$1.50	copies	$1.00

Please send me postpaid _____ copies of

The New Right: We're Ready to Lead. I enclose

$ _____

Payment in full must accompany order.

The Viguerie Company
7777 Leesburg Pike
Falls Church, Va. 22043

Order Form

THE NEW RIGHT: WE'RE READY TO LEAD

By Richard A. Viguerie

Introduction by Jerry Falwell

Order quantity copies of *The New Right: We're Ready to Lead* for your organization, your church, your club, your school, your friends. This dynamic book is filled with ideas and programs that can make America the Number One military power in the world again . . . put prayer back in our schools. . . protect our great Judeo-Christian heritage. . . reduce waste in government. . . preserve the American family. . .help you to be a more effective citizen. It's a book that can help make America great again.

Quantity Prices

1-9 copies	$2.25	100-499 copies	$1.25
10-24 copies	$1.90	500 or more	
25-99 copies	$1.50	copies	$1.00

Please send me postpaid _____ copies of

The New Right: We're Ready to Lead. I enclose

$ _____ .

Payment in full must accompany order.

The Viguerie Company
7777 Leesburg Pike
Falls Church, Va. 22043